STEP THIS WAY ...
MR LYNAM

THE GOOD, THE BAD & THE UGLY

STEP THIS WAY ...
MR LYNAM

THE GOOD, THE BAD & THE UGLY

Francis Ponder

Forewords by Tony English and Richard Wilkins

APEX PUBLISHING LTD

First published in hardback in 2016, then in paperback in 2016 by

Apex Publishing Ltd

12A St. John's Road, Clacton on Sea, Essex, CO15 4BP, United Kingdom

www.apexpublishing.co.uk

British Library Cataloguing-in-Publication Data
A catalogue record for this book
is available from the British Library

ISBN 978-1-911476-38-2

Typeset in 12pt Palatino Linotype

Production Manager: Chris Cowlin
Cover Design: Hannah Blamires
The Colchester United logo has been used by kind permission of
Colchester United Football Club

Publishers Note:
The views and opinions expressed in this publication are those of the author and are not necessarily those of Apex Publishing Ltd

Copyright:
Every attempt has been made to contact the relevant copyright holders, Apex Publishing Ltd would be grateful if the appropriate people contact us on: 01255 428500 or mail@apexpublishing.co.uk

In memory of my good friends
Peter Wright and John Brooke

CONTENTS

ACKNOWLEDGEMENTS

I dedicate this book to my lovely partner, Joanna Wright, the wonderful women in my life who encouraged me to put away my chef's hat and lawnmower to write this story.

I also dedicate my words to my son and daughter, Jamie and Marie, and my ex-wife, Liz, who all bore the brunt of my endless hours away from home covering the U's.

My thanks also go to my late mum, dad and older brother, Ivor, plus my other brothers, Roger and Adrian, and their families, who have all supported me along the way.

It would be very remiss of me not to applaud all my colleagues at Essex County Newspapers (ECN), from Peter Laurie, Peter Hills, Robin Frost and Peter Willis – who all made it happen for me – to all my good mates on the sports desk – Matt Plummer, Jonathan Waldron, Howard Walker, Mark Hayhurst, John Pakey, Simon Spurgeon, Vicki Hodges, Ian Oxborrow, Neil Thomas, David Hopps, Julie Lay, Martin Hunt, Graham Warwick, Ian Passingham, John Longman, Pete Long, Peter Jones, Martin Smith, Kim Mayo, Alex Martin and Derek Davis.

Special thanks go to all my other friends at ECN, especially the photographic team; Steve Brading, Terry Weeden, Steve Argent, Seana Hughes, Nigel Brown, Adrian Rushton and Warren Page, whose photographs enhance this book and portray the fun we all had at Layer Road and on our travels.

I recognise also the help and friendship I enjoyed with the *East Anglian Daily Times* Colchester United correspondents, Carl Marston and Neal Manning, plus BBC Essex football commentators Neil Kelly and Glenn Speller.

Lastly, but not least, my good friends at Colchester United and everyone connected with dear old Layer Road where I did all my reporting at home games.

Pictures reproduced courtesy of the *Colchester Daily Gazette* and *Essex County Standard*. Copyright is retained and any views expressed in this book are not necessarily shared by the titles. The Paul Gascoigne photograph is courtesy of Press Association Images.

AUTHOR'S NOTE

I have been a Colchester United fan all my life and I saw my first match at Layer Road back in February 1951.

It was Colchester's first season in the Football League Division Three (South) and my mum and dad took me along for a special treat.

The U's saw off Northampton Town two-one thanks to goals from Bob Curry and Johnny McKim.

I was only six-years-old, but I already had the football bug and almost every week thereafter I went along with my dad to watch the first team one week and the reserves the next.

The treat I always got afterwards was just as tasty as the matches. Dad and I walked up to the town centre where he always bought me a quarter of my favourite rum and butter toffees from the old Woolworths High Street store.

Back in those days, the U's were playing against Crystal Palace, Bournemouth and Watford – currently plying their trade in the Premier League – plus Nottingham Forest, Norwich City, Ipswich and Reading, who have all played in the top flight since then.

I saw mighty Arsenal held to an exciting two-all FA Cup draw in 1959, while nine months later north-eastern giants Newcastle United were humbled 4-1 in the Football League Cup with tiny Scottish wizard-of-dribble Sammy McLeod working his destructive magic.

Little did I know it then that around thirty years later I would not only be watching games involving the U's, I would be reporting on them for the *Colchester Evening*

Gazette. During my twenty-eight years with the paper I witnessed three Wembley finals, two promotions and two relegations.

This is a book about my *Gazette* experiences at Layer Road and on my travels up and down the country covering the team's exploits. More importantly, perhaps, it is a book about many of the stories I couldn't print in the paper.

Home and away I was doing my stuff from Plymouth down west to Carlisle and Hartlepool up north and travelling first with the fans, and then with the team, I made a lot of very good friends. I still see them now in the U's magnificent new home at the Weston Homes Community Stadium. One of my biggest regrets, however, is that I never got to report on a match in those wonderful new surroundings.

On reflection though, in this day and age of Twitter, Facebook and other instant social media that might not have been a bad thing. At least I reported at a time where I could actually watch the whole game and build relationships and contacts with the players instead of sitting in the Press Box, head down tapping away on a laptop keyboard in a bid to keep the sit-at-home fans informed.

Up the U's!
Francis Ponder

FOREWORD

Francis Ponder, 'The old Silver Fox'.

Someone who could destroy your weekend with a flick of his pen!

Francis (aka 'Frannie') was one of those rare breeds of reporters with whom I felt comfortable enough to attack his tie whenever in range; spike his tea with whatever I could get my hands on and generally abuse him, in a nice way (if that is possible).

I suppose it was our way of accepting him into the team, as it proved a few years later when he was allowed to travel on the team bus to away games.

Ah, away trips. I won't spoil some of the stories because I'm sure you will be reading about them soon (well, maybe not all of them).

Frannie took everything that was thrown at him (literally), but not once did I hear him moan, whine, whinge or complain to the manager – not that it would have made the slightest difference!

As a result, Frannie was quickly accepted by the players, most of them anyway – you can't please 'em all!

Best of luck Frannie with your new career as an author. I'm looking forward to reading the book – or should I be worried?

Tony English
Colchester United captain 1988–96

FOREWORD

I first met Francis Ponder in late 1986.

I was signed by Mike Walker for Colchester United, initially on non-contract forms after I had impressed him playing for Haverhill Rovers against the U's Reserves, who at the time played in the same League.

Frannie did a piece for the *Colchester Gazette* on my signing and seemed generally excited that I was a non-league player being provided with a great opportunity.

After I signed professionally I would often chat to Frannie on away trips about my second love – cricket.

My knowledge was somewhat over-shadowed by the silver haired wizard's name-dropping of famous Essex players that he spoke to regularly, Gooch, Foster and Fletcher, to name just a few.

What I found appealing was that Frannie was a genuine fan of Colchester United, he was frustrated over one game and overjoyed the next. I always found him honest and sincere and he had this beaming smile that always welcomed you.

I can remember a conversation we had during my second spell at the club, when the *Gazette* told him he had to give individual players a mark out of ten for each game. He was generally concerned about this and said he didn't feel he had the right or experience to mark players this way.

I told him that as long as the manager picked me I didn't give a monkey's what score he gave me. I can remember him laughing, although he sometimes got the cold shoulder from a few players who stupidly took it personally when he scored them low.

Frannie has witnessed the highs and lows at Colchester United over many a decade, but I can still see his face when we won promotion at Wembley in the play-off final against Torquay. His big infectious smile with tears of joy in his eyes.

For me, Frannie is a fantastic and knowledgeable person who dearly loves his passion for football and cricket.

He was always a total gentleman – a man with class!

Richard Wilkins
Colchester United captain 1997-2000

PROLOGUE

FRANCIS Ponder is one of a dwindling band whose support of Colchester United goes back to the club's first season in the Football League, 1950-51.

For sixty-six years, from his first match as a six-year-old at Layer Road, 'Frannie' has seen the highs and lows as the U's took fans to the heights of Championship football and three Wembley finals – and the lows of relegation out of the League and humiliating FA Cup defeats.

But it is his years as a football reporter for the *Colchester Evening Gazette* which makes this book special.

Francis Ponder joined the *Gazette* sports team in 1981 after being made redundant by the town's largest employer, Paxmans, where he had worked for sixteen years.

He rapidly became the newspaper's Essex County Cricket correspondent and wrote many stories involving Colchester United from 1985 onwards before, shortly after the start of the club's first season in the Conference (following relegation) in 1990-91, he took on the mantle as the official U's reporter.

What a journey he witnessed from the Conference back into the Football League with a FA Trophy victory at Wembley, two more Wembley appearances and the promotion to League One.

Francis handed over reporting the U's games in January 2005.

This book provides a unique insight into more about the U's during fifteen hectic and exciting seasons than any fan would know.

Observations and commentary from the inside knowledge he gleaned from being close to those directly involved in the club as it moved from the despair of relegation out of the Football League, to a journey of steady progress back and how the way was paved for eventual promotion to the Championship.

Francis Ponder's book is a must for all Colchester United supporters.

Sir Bob Russell
High Steward of Colchester

CHAPTER 1
THE DAY I BECAME COLCHESTER UNITED MANAGER

Friday, 30 October 1998 will remain vividly imprinted in my memory until the day I die.

It was the day I became Colchester United's manager!

The U's were preparing for their biggest match of the 1998-99 season against one of the biggest teams in the country, future Premier League champions, FA and League Cup winners, Manchester City, at their former Maine Road stadium.

As usual, I joined the team on the coach up north as we headed for our overnight stay in a hotel at the town of Hyde, Greater Manchester (mass-murderer Harold Shipman country).

The trip went well until we arrived outside the hotel late in the afternoon only to find a huge sign displaying the fact 'Friday Night is Ladies Night!'

U's boss Steve Wignall was spitting feathers. A hotel full of young women was the last thing he wanted before his team's biggest game of the season.

He would have been spitting even more feathers and tearing out his hair if he knew the unsavoury event that was about to unfold later that evening.

Everything was fine as we all sat down and enjoyed dinner and at 9 p.m. Wiggy, physio Brian Owen and the U's squad all went to their rooms for an early night to concentrate on their roles in the big match eighteen hours later.

That left me, kit manager John Brooke and four or five

others. We went for a drink and sat in the hotel foyer chatting when a group of girls decided to join us, parking themselves among us, intrigued as to who we were.

I was the only one not wearing a U's tracksuit and still wearing my collar and tie, with my greying moustache and distinguished white hair the girls immediately thought I was the team's manager – a lie that we all went along with.

Everything was fine until one of the girls took a real shine to a member of our party. He took a shine to her as well and we all moved into the disco where the pair of them danced together.

After a while, very late in the evening, we left the girls and went for another drink in the foyer. They came out soon after and joined us again at which point the girl in question said to the particular guy, "Why have you taken off your wedding ring?"

What happened next totally shocked and amazed us as he rose in a flash and crashed a sharp right-hander against the side of her face. He slapped her so hard it almost knocked her over!

We had to think quickly what to do to avoid a major incident and, with the girls looking at me as the 'would-be manager', I assured them that the guilty party would be severely punished, maybe thrown out of the club, when we returned to Colchester. They appeared happy with my explanation, but we went to bed that night wondering what the morning might have in store for us.

Luckily, some of the girls stayed overnight in the hotel as well, including the young lady in question, and when I ran into them after breakfast they were very happy with the action I told them we would be taking and were prepared to leave it at that.

Wiggy had no idea what had gone on that night. Neither did any of the board of directors.

God only knows what they would have done if they'd found out, but to this day I've not heard so much as a whisper of the unsavoury goings on in that hotel.

My short spell as the U's manager could have been a lot happier, but the team produced a good display when only going down 2-1 against the might of Manchester in front of a crowd of around 25,000.

CHAPTER 2
U'S – BOOZE – AND BIG BUST UP

Those of you who have read former Colchester United player and manager Roy McDonough's book* – *Red Card Roy* – will know that booze played a big part during his reign at Layer Road.

So it was on the night of Wednesday, 22 April 1992. Table-topping U's had just hammered Conference rivals Boston United 4-0 at their York Street stadium and, as was the tradition those days, the team stayed behind for a half hour or more to enjoy the odd pint or two.

My Gazette newsroom colleague, Paul 'Middo' Middleton, had been allowed to make the trip on the team coach with me and all was well as we headed out of Lincolnshire on the road back to Colchester. Everyone was in a buoyant mood as the Conference title beckoned with just three more games to play and some of the players brought their beer back on the coach to celebrate the latest big win.

One of those players was towering midfielder Dave Martin who was on loan from Essex neighbours Southend United in a bid to get match fit following a career-threatening injury. Big Dave, who had clearly already had one too many, plonked himself down – pint glass in hand – in the seat facing me and Middo.

Paul enquired how come Martin came to be with Colchester at which I pointed out that the Shrimpers stalwart was recovering from a nasty knee injury and was with the U's as he strived to regain full fitness. Heaven only knows what Dave thought I had said, but the colour suddenly drained from his face as he

4

threatened to rub his pint glass in my kisser.

McDonough, who was sitting on the other side of the coach to us, saw that the drunken Martin meant to cause trouble and promptly stepped in to quieten things down with the threat, "Behave yourself, Dave, or you won't be going to Wembley!"

Martin was having none of it, however, and threw the remains of his beer in McDonough's face, at the same time threatening to 'smash' my f*****g face in before he got off the coach.

God only knows what Middo was thinking – taking evasive action under the table if he had any sense! As for me – I was shitting myself. I'd never seen anyone so mad. Martin's face was ashen. He had a real evil look in his eyes and his actions were very frightening. I honestly thought I was going to have a broken glass pushed into my ugly mug or, at the very least, cop a bloody good-hiding.

To his credit, Big Roy kept as cool as a cucumber and assured me that everything was going to be all right as long as I remained on the coach when we arrived back at Layer Road.

Everything did turn out all right and, as I was set to miss the next match away at Macclesfield, which coincided with my 48th birthday, I wasn't going to meet up with Dave Martin again until the following Tuesday when the U's entertained Kettering Town in their penultimate game of the season.

When I made my customary phone call to the club that morning for some team news, I was told to report to the dressing room before the match, but I had no idea why.

Roy welcomed me inside where big Dave put his arm around my shoulder and, in front of everyone, duly apologised for his disgraceful behaviour on the journey back from Boston. Footballers aren't good at doing that sort of thing and it was really big of Dave to declare his remorse so openly. He went up a lot in my estimation for doing that and two weeks later he turned in a man-of-the-match starring performance as the U's clinched the second leg of their Conference and FA Trophy winning double with a 3-1 win over Witton Albion in the Wembley final.

The book 'Red Card Roy' – superbly written by my good friend and 'Daily Mirror' journalist Bernie Friend – is still available from bookshops and Amazon.

CHAPTER 3
PERSONA NON GRATA

My relationship with U's chairman Peter Heard was, to say the least, tempestuous at the best of times.

Mr Chairman, as he was always known to me, (he always called me Mr Ponder) and I seldom saw eye-to-eye and, although we both loved the club, he would never realise that my job as the Evening Gazette's Colchester United correspondent meant I had to ask the questions the fans wanted answers to – a fact he didn't always like.

Before I go any further let me stress I had the greatest admiration and respect for Mr Heard. When the club's future was thrown into jeopardy following relegation out of the Football League at the end of the 1989-90 season, he put his hands deep into his pockets to bankroll continued full-time professional football at Layer Road. Had he not done that one is left to wonder – would there still be a Colchester United today, or would the U's have disappeared off the radar altogether?

However, the annoying thing on my part was the fact that, right from the outset, he told me that U's Secretary-cum-Chief Executive, Marie Partner, was his eyes, ears and mouthpiece at the club and I should contact her for any information.

Invariably, all too often she would say to me, "I'll have to check with the chairman first." That was no good to me because Mr Heard always went for a morning swim and would never return to his office until after my deadline – I had a paper to get out!

A very quiet and private man in his day-to-day life, had 'Mr Chairman' made himself available maybe some of the stories he didn't like would have been different. That said, I'll never forget the game at Stoke City's Britannia Stadium on Saturday, 26 September 2001 when I did get to speak to him face to face.

I had just taken my seat high up in the main stand as the match summarizer next to BBC Essex football commentator Neil Kelly, when I noticed the chairman and fellow U's director, Peter Powell, scouring the heights as if they were looking for someone.

That someone turned out to be me, because when the half-time whistle sounded Mr Heard climbed over the barriers surrounding the directors' box and headed upwards, obviously straight towards me. I could hardly believe my eyes and ears at what happened next. Trembling with rage, and/or nervous energy, he put a hand inside his coat pocket for, what turned out to be, a wad of letters.

"Are you trying to destroy my club?" he asked, clearly upset, with a tear or two rolling down his cheeks.

What the hell's this all about? I thought to myself. Me, a one-time snotty nosed kid from a council house in Tolleshunt D'Arcy, has reduced this self-made millionaire to a quivering wreck.

I told him Colchester United was my club as well.

He promptly hit back with the spiteful gibe, "The trouble with you, Mr Ponder, is your mouth is always open and your wallet is always closed, whereas my mouth is always closed and my wallet is always open."

What a bloody daft thing to say!

The U's results had been up and down for some time and every Monday morning three or four fans would ring up the *Gazette* to have a moan and ask me what was going on.

"You must know," they said. "You travel on the team coach, know what the tactics are and even help to pick the team!"

"Don't be silly," I told them. "I only travel with the squad. I'm not privy to anything to do with the team. Why don't you write to the manager or chairman if you're not happy." They clearly took me at my word and let the chairman know that I had told them to do it!

There was no pacifying 'Mr Chairman' whatever I said to him. He was convinced I was out to stir up trouble for him and the club.

"Whatever did you say to Peter Heard on Saturday?" Marie Partner asked in a phone call to me the following Monday. "He was shaking like a leaf when he left you. I had to hold his hand to try and calm him down all through the second half!

"You're a couple of silly sods," she went on. "You both want what is best for the club, but you come at it from different angles."

I was well aware a long while before that little spat, that you were 'persona non grata' (an unwelcome person) if you didn't sing from the same song sheet as Mr Heard.

I wasn't the only one who fell foul of Mr Chairman's philosophies. Manager Phil Parkinson suffered a bit of his 'cold shoulder' treatment when he was being chased by several clubs after guiding the U's up into the Championship in 2005-06 – the highest the team had ever been in their long history.

The chairman had put a block on the likes of Hull City, Charlton Athletic, Ipswich Town and Derby County speaking to Parky, fact or rumour, the former Reading midfielder wasn't too happy about. Parky was so incensed that he phoned me from an airport in Greece (where he was holidaying with his family) one Sunday lunchtime and said: "The chairman and Marie Partner aren't answering my phone calls. Can you tell them if they don't I will tell the press what is going on at Layer Road."

Bloody hell, I thought. I've got a bit of a scoop here, but then it dawned on me that I was being used.

I promptly phoned my editor and asked, "What do you want me to do?"

"Go along with it and phone Marie while I phone the club's general manager," came the reply.

I duly phoned Marie to deliver Parky's ultimatum and, as you may have already guessed, the phone line was red-hot between Colchester and Greece that afternoon.

Parky must have been happy with what he heard because I didn't get my exclusive. What I could have done was not bother to have alerted the club of Parky's 'blackmail' threat so that I could get my scoop. Marie and 'Mr Chairman' were not aware of that possibility of course!

A few days later, following more back-biting and bitterness between Mr Heard and Hull City chairman, Adam Pearson, compensation of between £400,000 and £600-000 was agreed between the two clubs and Parky became the Tigers manager. Parkinson, meanwhile, wasn't the first U's manager to suffer the cold shoulder treatment from the club's hierarchy.

Chairman at the time, Gordon Parker, and the U's board of directors – including Peter Heard, who generally controlled the purse strings – denied Steve Wignall the opportunity to speak with Brentford, who were seeking his services, after he had guided the U's to the Auto Windscreens Shield final at Wembley in the

1996-97 season.

Wiggy was equally incensed the following season when, with the U's only ninety minutes away from an automatic promotion spot in the former Division Three, with just three games to play, the U's board of directors refused the team an overnight hotel stay in Chester, forcing them instead to travel up to the Welsh border (a round trip of 451 miles) on the day.

Tired, stiff and weary from an early morning start and the long journey, a lethargic and wooden U's were soundly beaten, 3-1, by their mid-table rivals at the Deva Stadium.

That escapade prompted me to suggest the headline – Professionalism = preparation = passion = points = prizes = PROMOTION! Yet another Ponder story Mr Heard, Mr Parker and their fellow directors didn't like!

Thankfully the U's did go on to achieve promotion via the play-offs, defeating Torquay United by a David Gregory penalty in a Friday night Wembley final.

It might have been so much better had Wiggy and the boys enjoyed that disallowed overnight stay. As it turned out, they finished the season only one point away from the three automatic promotion places.

Mr Heard also had a bee in his bonnet about not rewarding players over thirty-years-of-age with a two-year contract. This rebounded on him in the summer of 2004 when popular club captain and recently crowned U's Player of the Year, Alan White, made a shock departure to Third Division Leyton Orient.

When 'Mr Chairman' was told the news he promptly offered the fans' favourite a new two-year deal, but a man of principle, White spurned the offer stating at the time that he had already shaken hands on his new contract with O's chairman, Barry Hearn. The U's boss at the time, Phil Parkinson, said to me that he and the chairman didn't like my story. I told Parky that I didn't write them for him or Mr Heard. I write them for the fans.

'Mr Chairman' blew another fuse three years later when top marksmen Jamie Cureton and Chris Iwelumo – forty-two goals between them in the season – accused the club of lacking the same ambition as they had.

They, too, were seeking new two-year deals having initially only been offered one, and I remember writing, 'Most clubs in a similar position would be looking to build their team around two such prolific scorers as Player of the Year Cureton and Iwelumo.'

Championship Golden Boot winner Cureton moved on to one of his former clubs, Norwich City, for a transfer fee of £825-000, while free agent Iwelumo joined recently relegated Premier League club Charlton Athletic.

I was reliably informed by a good source within the club there was no way Colchester could match the lucrative deal Charlton were offering Iwelumo.

'Mr Chairman' dished out more of his wrath in my direction earlier in the year when club captain Karl Duguid, who enjoyed writing a weekly column for charity in the *Gazette,* handed me another exclusive back page splash sporting the headline – PAY US WHAT WE DESERVE – following the £2.5 million transfer of utility man Greg Halford to Premier League club Reading.

Dugy claimed that some of that cash should have been spent on enhancing the current squad's contracts.

"We are Championship footballers now," he said "And having done so well in our first season at that level everyone should be rewarded for the good job they have done."

I was told 'Mr Chairman' saw red and was spitting

feathers with me and Dugy. He stopped Dugy from doing the column and threatened to take the captaincy away from him.

However, the snub that beat all snubs for me came down at Yeovil on the day the U's clinched promotion to the Championship – the final match of the 2005-06 season. I had already relinquished my role as the *Gazette*'s U's correspondent because of my two full knee-replacement operations, but agreed to help the lads out.

At the end of the match I got within arm's-length of Mr Chairman, who was conducting an interview with my *East Anglian Daily Times* rival Derek Davis. When I stepped up to speak to him, Mr Heard called over the U's media officer, David Gregory, to inform me that he was not doing any more interviews with the press that day. How bloody childish!

I would have thought more of him if he'd had the balls to look me in the eye and tell me that himself. I can take on the chin the fact that 'Mr Chairman' didn't particularly like me, but the very supportive *Gazette* deserved a lot better than it got down at Yeovil that day.

However, my relationship with 'Mr Chairman' has sweetened somewhat since then. The pressures of running a football club lifted from his shoulders have revealed the nice, very likeable bloke Mr Heard really is, while I hope the same can be said of me now that the suspicions surrounding constant scavenging for stories have been erased following my retirement.

Despite everything I have revealed in this chapter I have to admit that, under the stewardship of Peter 'The Referee' Heard and his fellow directors, John 'The Jam' Worsp, Peter 'Legal Beagle' Powell and Gordon 'Bob The Builder' Parker, the U's rose from the obscurity of the GM Vauxhall Conference into the Football League

Championship.

A great job well done – and to his credit, putting all the wrath and red mists aside, 'Mr Chairman' never once put a block on me speaking to the U's manager or the players.

The lifelong U's supporter that I am, it would have been so easy to make excuses for the club and write about them through rose-tinted glasses. However, as I have always maintained, if you are going to do a job, do it properly and that's what I always set out to do!

CHAPTER 4
FIERY JOCK HAD A SURPRISE
OR TWO IN STORE

I never really believed all the rumours that chairman
Jonathan Crisp was hounding legendary Glasgow
Rangers manager Jock Wallace to become beleaguered
Colchester United's new boss in place of Roger Brown.
But he did, Jock came and conquered and retained the
U's status as a Football League club.

Typical of the man, Jock arrived on 12 January 1989
and his clenched-fist image, powerful rallying call, along
with the *Evening Gazette*'s SOS – Save Our Soccer –
campaign made an immediate impact on the club and
the town.

The U's were bottom of the old Fourth Division at the
time and in grave danger of being relegated out of the
Football League. Forsaking the Spanish sunshine for the
English winter, proud speaking Jock promptly worked
his magic and with Layer Road crowds soaring from just
over 1,500 to 5,250, Wallace's battlers went into the final
game of the season knowing their Division Four survival
was already safe.

The big Scot had been visibly shaken several weeks
earlier following the Hillsborough disaster which
claimed the lives of 96 Liverpool fans in the FA Cup
semi-final against Nottingham Forest.

What happened next left me shocked and completely
stunned, for Jock phoned me early on the Monday after
and said: "If you want to speak to me today get your arse
down to the ground 'cos I'm not talking to you over the

phone."

I thought to myself: *Hello! He's not happy with the 1-1 draw at Lincoln City the previous Saturday.*

I'd already decided to ask him – should some of the big money being spent on transfers be channelled into ground safety instead following the Hillsborough tragedy?

When I got to Layer Road Jock seated me on the opposite side of a table to him and, when I put my question to him, he rose suddenly, as if in a rage, turning the table over on me and with the colour draining from his face, he roared in his broad East Lothian accent, "If yeh gorn te continye thut laine oh questyenin ye cun f**k-off noo." We stared at each other for what seemed an eternity, when Jock said to me, "Sit down son. I'll answer your question."

Clearly upset, he did answer my question, but not before he pointed out: "I'm sorry son, but what happened at Hillsborough on Saturday has left me plainly dejected and filled with sorrow. I feel empty and share the grief and emotion with the Liverpool people."

Jock had already experienced a similar tragedy in the 1971 Ibrox Stadium disaster in Glasgow where a crash barrier gave way at the end of an 'old firm' derby between Rangers and Celtic in which sixty-six people lost their lives.

He went on, "What happened at Hillsborough brought the memories of Ibrox flooding back to me and I was glad I was on my own as I watched that FA Cup tragedy unfold.

"I'll never forget the scenes of bodies and injured people being brought into the Ibrox dressing rooms and the vain attempts at resuscitation.

"Glasgow lost a lot of good people and Rangers and

Celtic lost a lot of fans.

"I went to four funerals after that game and it has left me shaken and deeply scarred."

However, he insisted, "What happened has happened and the best way to get over the tragedy is to get playing again.

"They didn't stop playing after the Rangers and Celtic disaster and they didn't stop playing after the Munich disaster, the Heysel Stadium disaster, the fire at Bradford City and life didn't stop after the bombs on Hiroshima.

"We must get playing again as quickly as possible – the game of football must go on!"

With rumours rife that Jock was by now suffering from the early stages of Parkinson's disease, performances in the new season began to plummet again, but I wasn't ready for what Jock had in store for me on Wednesday morning, 20 December 1989.

I went to the ground as usual for Jock's team news for that evening's Leyland DAF Trophy outing at Maidstone when he handed me the shock news and *Gazette* front and back page scoop: "It's not me you need to be talking to. Steve Foley is in charge!"

News of Wallace's resignation wasn't officially due to be released until later in the week, but typical of Big Jock's gruff honesty he let the cat out of the bag. He told me, "The official announcement will come later, but I'm not beating about the bush! The fans and people connected with the club deserve better, so Steve Foley is taking over as caretaker manager from today.

"I won't be quitting the club altogether, but I think the time is right for the team to go in a different direction with a fresh manager. In my role as a director I will remain very much involved in the recruitment of new players.

"There has been a pride and a passion about the place," said Jock "And that wonderful feeling will remain with me forever!"

"He is a very good man," said U's chairman Jonathan Crisp.

CHAPTER 5
DOPPELGANGER DES?

It's so often said that each and every one of us has a Doppelganger somewhere on this earth.

If all the evidence is to be believed, my doppelganger is the famous television personality we all know – Desmond Lynam!

I personally can't see the likeness, although I have got grey hair and I did sport a moustache, but I've been called his name so many times there must be something in it.

A Lay & Wheeler workmate of my ex-wife was the first to call me Des and it just snowballed from there.

I distinctly recall walking up Colchester's North Hill from the *Gazette* office one lunchtime when a guy came running up from behind me, stopped about five yards in front and shouted to his friends, "It is him, it's not him – I'm not sure though."

But the fact that I did look like Des was really brought home to me when the U's played Witton Albion in the FA Trophy final at Wembley. Roy McDonough had arranged an official pass for me to join the team in the dressing room and when I wandered round to the big doors leading to the changing area and players tunnel a female steward took one look at me and said, "Step this way, Mr Lynam!"

I didn't even have to show her my pass.

However, fact turned to fiction when a few of my *Gazette* colleagues suggested I looked more like actor Ronald Forfar – you know that bedraggled looking father figure, Freddie Boswell, in the TV sitcom *Bread*.

CHAPTER 6
HIGH SPIRITS ON THE BUSES

There was never a dull moment on the team coach as the Colchester United squad travelled the length and breadth of the country to play their GM Vauxhall Conference and Football League soccer.

With early morning starts to such places as Barrow and Gateshead, plus Carlisle and Hartlepool, the U's squad had more than enough time on their hands to find something to keep them occupied. There was music and laughter, high spirits and fun abound. We must have watched every sitcom from *Only Fools and Horses* to *Fawlty Towers*, all the best films from *Brassed Off* to *Braveheart* and when none of that was going on, some poor sod, somewhere on the coach, was being put through the ringer.

Throughout all of my times travelling on the team coach I always informed the respective U's managers that I 'reserved the right to criticise the team's performances when they played badly' – an observation that was received very well – maybe not by all the players!

My first vivid memory of the high jinks and fun came on the U's trip to table-topping Farnborough, fifteen games into the second season of Conference football. Goals from Gary Bennett and Shaun Elliott had deservedly earned Roy McDonough's squad a fine 2-0 win, a win which hoisted them above The Yellows to the top where they were never to be headed again.

Stoked up by a few bevies and endless cans of amber nectar, the coach journey home was soon rocking to the sound of raucous Irish folk songs ably conducted and loudly sung by a very happy Dublin duo Eamonn Collins and Mark Kinsella.

I was initially invited to travel with the team by player-manager Ian Atkins, but it was under Big Roy's wing that I first copped a few mud pies. You definitely needed to keep your wits about you at all times and, as 'The Outsider' in the pack, I knew I was always going to be fair game for the jokers.

I made the mistake of nodding off on one journey home only to find my shoelaces tied together when I woke and attempted to get up. Everyone sitting around me looked so innocent but, as I was later to find to my cost, no-one was safe while Tony 'Squid' English, Nicky 'Smudger' Smith, Mark 'Sheedy' Kinsella and Simon 'Bettsy' Betts were around. If it wasn't shoe laces with a million knots tied in them it would more than likely be coffee grains and sugar sprinkled in my hair.

I was dead beat and frankly out on my feet on another trip home and made the fatal mistake of dropping off to sleep again only to wake up and find one of the pockets of my £600.00 leather jacket stuffed full of cold cod (the leftovers of a couple of players' meals) while the pocket on the other side was overflowing with coffee grains and sugar.

"You f**king load of bastards," I yelled at the mischief-making 'Double Duo.'

"Don't look at us," they said, trying to disguise their laughter.

But the icing on the cake for 'Smudger' and 'Squid' came after the final game of the U's first season back in the Football League. We were making our way back home from Wrexham when 'Big Roy' allowed the lads to nip into a roadside supermarket and fill up with sandwiches, choc bars, nuts, sweets and fizzy pop.

The coach hadn't been back on the road very long when young players Gary Bennett and Martin Grainger started to chuck nuts, Mars bars, Bounty bars, Twixes and Crunchie bars across the bus at each other.

I had made the trip smartly dressed in collar, tie, slacks and blazer as I was due to go to a party when I got back. So I thought quickly to myself *I'd better get out of the firing line here* and, leaving my blazer behind, I secretly (so I thought) sneaked out of danger into the back seat.

Sadly for me, 'Smudger' and 'Squid' had spotted my little ruse and a moment later all hell was let loose. Shaving cream, chocolate, bottles of water, the filling of a sandwich or two, nuts, crisps, toothpaste and a couple of two-litre bottles of cherryade were emptied over my head.

I looked like a proper drowned rat, more like a drenched scarecrow than a smart party-goer, but with the entire coach roaring their heads off I knew it was useless to react, so I laughed along with them only to cop another load of piss-taking on my return home.

Travelling with the team had its great advantages too. I got to see the inside of many opponents' dressing rooms when helping physio Brian Owen and kit manager John Brooke lay-out the players' gear and boots. I was also right on the spot five games into the 1999-2000 season when the coach home from Selhurst Park was delayed by an hour, only to learn chairman Peter Heard had installed Steve Whitton as U's boss in place of Mick Wadsworth. I climbed into the coach expecting to write about a Worthington Cup defeat at the hands of Crystal Palace only to be handed a *Gazette* back page exclusive full of Whitts' quotes.

Lady luck was on my side when I was 'Johnny on the Spot' again less than a year later as we boarded the coach home from another Worthington Cup outing to Sheffield United. Rumours were rife of a multi-million pound transfer of Lomana Tresor Lua Lua to Newcastle United and on the way up to Bramall Lane Steve Whitton asked me not to pester the player.

I honoured Whitts' request and, as I boarded the coach to come home, he told me a deal had all but been done, you can speak to Lomana now – yet another following day *Gazette* "I'M OFF TO JOIN MY HERO!" (Alan Shearer) exclusive.

I was also there when serious injuries delayed our journey home. The first was way back in September 1995 when Steve Whitton sustained a cruciate ligament injury following a wicked and crude unpunished high tackle by Darlington's Sean Gregan. We had to wait while the Darlington Memorial Hospital stabilised Whitts' knee enough for him to travel home.

A similar fate awaited Karl Duguid at Boundary Park, Oldham where he was ferried off to the Royal Infirmary on a stretcher with his neck in a brace following a heavy tackle. A journey round to the hospital found Dugy in good spirits.

The worst looking injury of the lot was suffered by fullback Joe Dunne at Kenilworth Road, Luton. Joe took the full impact of Matthew Taylor's six studs in his face, a horrific injury that could have cost him an eye, but left him with forty stitches in a wound by the side of his right ear. Poor old Joe looked a right mess when we picked him up from the Luton and Dunstable Hospital.

I was in a right mess the day I missed the supporters' coach to Bournemouth, but Colchester taxi driver, Richard, came to the rescue and drove me down to Dean Court. The U's fans never let me forget it on the way home. God only knows how much that trip cost the *Gazette*, but I never heard another thing about it.

On a brighter note, I enjoyed some of the finest spaghetti bolognese I've ever tasted thanks to Steve Wignall's on-coach chef, Magical Martyn Gosling.

I both started and finished my U's reporting on the supporters' coach, where I enjoyed some equally great journeys and met some wonderful people, not to mention some fantastic coach drivers.

On the driver front there was Graham and Paul Layzell, George and Barry Osborne, Kevin Haye, Ivor Reynolds, Bob Snow, Tony Partridge and Tim Rampling.

The super U's fans included Jon Burns, Jeanette and Roger Westlake, Jackie and Robbie Anderson, Keith and Lynda Brandon, Peter and Jean Coe, Mary and Coral Wightman, Pat and Les Oakes, Richard and Robin Fisher, Laura Sheldrake, Trevor Bailey, Chris Hazlehurst, John Tweed, Phil 'The Denim Dude' Gladwin – every one of them a real diamond. Special mention goes to my friend, Margaret Goodwin. Thanks for all the lifts home Margaret! Great to have met you all folks.

There was also one particularly sad and emotional coach journey for me, Mansfield away on Saturday, 2 April 1994. My wife at the time, Liz, informed me just before midnight the night before that she had fallen in love with another man and our marriage was over – I felt like a real April fool then!

I had no chance of getting someone to stand-in for me so I had no alternative but to join the U's fans and make the trip – professional to the last!

Miserable sod that I was that day I don't think I said a word to anyone and I couldn't wait to get back home that night just to be with myself.

CHAPTER 7
FUN AND GAMES

One thing the U's players could always be relied upon for – was to have a lot of FUN!

It was never difficult getting them to make fools of themselves by dressing up as a pantomime cow, Father Christmas, the Three Wise Men, or something equally as daft as that.

I remember the 1997 Christmas Eve edition of the *Gazette* where we persuaded the Mercury Theatre to loan us some costumes, including a pantomime cow. What a laugh me and the lads had. Mark Sale and David Gregory climbed into the pantomime cow, defender Scott Stamps cut a dashing figure as a panto dame while future manager Joe Dunne, ace marksman Tony Adcock and young midfielder David Rainford frolicked around in girls dresses – lipstick and all. Panto time at Layer Road made a very colourful and entertaining page and a half spread.

In a similar vein, manager Steve Wignall, Tony Adcock and Micky Cook sported long white wigs and beards to portray three 'Golden Oldies' or the Three Wise Men. Steve Whitton donned a Roman centurion's outfit, sword and shield to boot, to celebrate his 100th appearance for the U's.

"You'll never get him to do it," said his mum and dad!

We dressed the Gregory brothers, David and Neil, in top hats, tails, bow ties and brollies, courtesy of Colchester Menswear shop Jolliffes, to mark the fact they at one time both played for Peterborough whose nickname was 'The Posh.'

Too many cooks do spoil the broth as Devilish duo Peter Cawley and Mark Sale proved when they donned the garb of a couple of head chefs, including the toques – white high hats. Commercial comics John Shultz and Brian Wheeler cut great figures as Laurel and – that's another fine mess you've got me into – Hardy!

Popular goalkeeper Andy Woodman dressed up as a clown, gold bowler hat, big red nose, green tinsel hair and giant blue and white spotted bow tie for a 'Guess whose birthday it is' competition.

Leicester City loanee, Guy 'Caveman' Branston, really got into a pickle when we contacted Crosse and Blackwell – makers of the famous Branston Pickle brand. They sent us a giant six-pack of their tasty relish and big Guy couldn't wait to tuck into it. It made a great back page picture.

Meanwhile, popular groundsman and stadium manager, David Blacknall, was led a merry dance by a cunning fox in the stillness of the night on match days at the U's old Layer Road ground. 'Old Red' used to sneak out from his lair under one of the floodlight pylons at the top end of the ground to bury under the centre-spot partly eaten hamburgers he had scavenged around the stadium long after all the fans had gone home.

I don't know whether David ever caught him, or not? What a laugh!

CHAPTER 8
EVERY CLOUD HAS A
SILVER LINING

There's an old saying in life – every cloud has a silver lining!

That was certainly the case when I set out on my incredible journey into journalism. At the ripe old age of thirty-seven, married with a mortgage and two children, I suddenly found myself treading a path in life that, before, I could only dream about.

I was about to become a sports journalist with the *Colchester Evening Gazette* at Essex County Newspapers. When I left school at fifteen-years-old without a qualification to my name I didn't give a career in journalism a single thought. All I ever wanted to do was play football and cricket and, although I progressed to a decent level, sadly I was nowhere near good enough at either of those sports.

Mum insisted that I embarked on an engineering apprenticeship, even though I hated the sight of metalwork and woodwork at school. As it turned out I launched my working career in horticultural engineering with the Heybridge firm of E. H. Bentall.

On completing my six years of what I still call cheap-labour, winning the coveted prize of East Anglian Apprentice of the Year in my field along the way, I left for pastures new to try my hand at diesel engineering with the famous Colchester company Davey Paxman.

Answering an SOS call to return to Bentalls, a move that didn't really work-out for me, I spent the rest of my engineering life back at Paxmans until a surprise redundancy, along with eighty-seven workmates, in the autumn of 1980, sent my world crashing around my feet. *What the hell do I do now?* I asked myself.

If I wanted to continue in the line of work I was apprenticed to it would have meant pulling up sticks and moving my family up north, or into the Midlands. I was very reluctant to do that.

I thought this was the ideal time to get out of factory life, but I didn't have a clue where or when, or what doing. As things turned out, I needn't have worried because, on the very day I was officially made redundant, a phone call out of the blue – my cloud with a silver lining – was to set me on a career that as a school kid I could only have dreamt about.

I had only been indoors five minutes – after going into Paxmans to collect my P45 and redundancy pay-off – when Peter Willis, the editor of the *Maldon and Burnham Standard*, telephoned seeking information about the Maldon Sunday Football League (sadly now defunct).

"Why are you ringing me?" I asked. "Why aren't you calling the League's press officer?"

"He's useless," replied Peter, "I'm ringing you because as a previous press officer I know you will tell me what I want to know."

I had been the Maldon Sunday League press officer for two or three years earlier, making sure that my copy, results, updated tables and fixtures were always in the paper's Colchester office by lunchtime on Monday.

After furnishing Mr Willis with the information he was seeking I simply chanced my luck and asked, "You wouldn't have any jobs going would you?"

"What do you mean," he replied.

"I've just been made redundant and am looking for a

new job," I said.

To which he replied, "Are you serious?"

"I couldn't be more serious," I responded and he promptly told me I could be just the man he was looking for as long as I was prepared to do other work as well as sport.

"Give me the chance," I said, and that's how my new role in life began.

It was a Tuesday afternoon when Peter rang me, the day before the *M&B Standard* went to press.

"Leave it with me because I have to make another phone call," he said and, within the half-hour, he was back on the line.

"Are you free tomorrow because I'll pick you up and show you around the press," he said.

Little did I know then that he had also arranged an interview for me with Peter Hills, Essex County Newspapers' acting Editorial Director, for later that same afternoon.

Everything obviously went well because two days later I received a letter informing me that I could start at the *Maldon and Burnham* two weeks later.

Sadly, it all went pear-shaped after that because I received another letter informing me there was no longer a place for me in the paper – I would have to re-apply for a job as an adult entrant. I duly sent in my application only to be bombed out again because I didn't possess the necessary journalistic skills. The bottom dropped out of my world at that point and, after talking things over with my wife, she said, "You'll have to do something."

Every job I applied for ran up against a brick wall and, having given up all hope of working in the newspaper, I received another phone call out of the blue in early January 1981 – four months after my engineering career hit the rocks. This call was from Peter Laurie, editor of the *Evening Gazette,* enquiring if I was still interested in joining the paper's sports team.

"You bet I am," I excitedly replied, and within a few days he was welcoming me in his office and introducing me to my new boss, *Gazette* sports editor Robin Frost.

Believe it or not I still had a few hurdles to jump, none bigger than the NUJ (National Union of Journalists) Father of the Chapel (union shop steward in other words) who insisted that I started like a school leaver on a school leaver's pay.

"I can't do that with the best will in the world," I said and went home that night believing yet another door had just been slammed in my face.

However, Peter Laurie called me again and told me that with my knowledge of the local sports scene I was the man he wanted and, unbeknown to the Father of the Chapel, Peter said, "We operate a weekly expenses scheme here and if you bring your expenses form to me every Friday we'll make up your pay to a living wage.

I have never enjoyed so many fictitious lunches, suppers and travelling expenses in my life and with the outstanding support of my wife, her family and mine, we made it work.

I had always been a strong union man all my working life and was amazed when the very thing I believed in was not prepared to support me at a time when I most wanted it to.

I had the greatest of pleasure in telling the Father of the Chapel to stick his union form where the sun doesn't shine. "You're not getting any money out of me," I boldly told him. I knew he headed a load of gutless wonders because the journos had just returned to work without any improvement in pay or conditions, following a six-week strike.

So began the most exciting chapter in my working life. If I couldn't play football and cricket for a living, being involved in the sports in some way was the next best thing.

I had never typed a word when I started and learned the job as I went along. I went on to meet some of the biggest household names in sport during the next twenty-eight years, until my retirement on my 65th birthday, 25 April 2009.

I became the paper's official Essex County Cricket correspondent early in my journalistic career, taking in several County Championship titles and Lord's Cup finals.

Although I had interviewed several Layer Road managers and players and already written the odd match report, I only landed my dream job six games into the U's first season of GM Vauxhall Conference football – I was now the *Gazette*'s official Colchester United correspondent.

CHAPTER 9
ON YOUR MARKS

The worst thing the national newspapers ever did was to start marking players performances in matches. It meant provincial papers like the *Colchester Evening Gazette* had to follow suit.

I argued with the *Gazette*'s editor that it was okay for the nationals because they had the entire Premier and Football League clubs to upset, while I had to face the U's players every week. I didn't mind selecting a Player of the Match, but I felt that marking the players out of ten and, describing their performances in a sentence, would put an unnecessary strain on our working relationship and was a recipe for disaster.

As it turned out, I needn't have worried. I think most of the U's players didn't give a damn what I thought and took the whole exercise in their stride.

Only three players ever questioned their marks. Central defender Paul Roberts was the first when I only gave him a three following a stinker of a display in a Tuesday night debacle at Darlington. Robbo was atrocious. He never put a foot right all night and, despite the horrendous 7-3 scoreline, only the brilliance of U's goalkeeper John Keeley kept him out of jail many other times on the night.

I thought to myself, *bloody hell, what's Robbo going to say when he sees me in a few days' time?*

The U's next opponents were Walsall and before the match Robbo – who had a big reputation for being a joker – approached me and asked, "Where the f**k did you get three marks from, Francis?"

I thought quickly and replied, "One for turning up; another for looking smart and the third simply for being on the pitch!"

Expecting a mouthful of abuse back, he looked at me, laughed his head off and said: "Christ, you over-marked me by three. I was shit all night and expected to get hauled out of it at any time!"

Robbo's response was completely different to that of U's crowd-pleaser Sam Stockley, in a game during manager Phil Parkinson's reign at Layer Road. Sam was incensed, and so was Parky, after I gave the defender a mark of only four in a game where he hit a poorly directed pass which led directly to a goal for the opposition and later, in my opinion, made pretend he had been knocked out sparko, arms akimbo as he lay flat-out on his back in the U's penalty area, which led directly to a further goal for the opponents.

"I don't like it," said Parky on the phone. "I don't want my players upset when I'm trying to keep the squad happy and together."

"I don't care what you or Sam think," I responded. "If I'm having to mark players I'm going to do it as I see it. I'm not going to make excuses for anyone. If I was your player you would have expected a better display from me than Sam gave you and, if I had done my job as badly as Sam, my editor would have kicked my arse big time."

Parky accepted my explanation and so did Sam when he phoned minutes later.

I told him why I had given him a mark of four and added, "If you had been genuinely knocked out like you pretended you were, there's no way you could have got up and played on as if nothing had happened. I've been knocked out playing football and I didn't know where I was for a long time.

"Your fake injury – put on for the fans – and your earlier bad pass, both led to goals and I would have hauled you off the pitch for performing so poorly!"

I think my explanation shocked Sam a bit and he didn't make another murmur.

He was great about it afterwards and never bore any grudges. I liked Sam a lot.

The other culprit was often under-rated midfielder David Gregory whose typical response to low marks was always, "How many League games have you played then?" as if I knew nothing about football.

To be fair to Gregors, the nature of a football reporter's job means he has to keep his eye on the ball and where the action is. He doesn't always see what is happening elsewhere on the pitch.

I learned a lot later that if the manager wanted a particular job done, such as marking the opposition's danger-man out of the game, that task was often allotted to Gregors. Successful as he might have been at this, his exploits only too often went unnoticed by we hacks up in the press box.

As far as describing a player's performance goes? Trying to write something different in a sentence while marking players was harder sometimes than compiling the match report itself.

CHAPTER 10
HEARTS OF GOLD

Anyone who supported Colchester United during Roy McDonough's reign as a player and manager will be very aware that 'Big Mac' had as many enemies as friends.

For those who idolised him like a god Roy could do no wrong, while those who loathed him were only too ready to condemn him before he had even set foot out of the dressing room.

I didn't agree with everything he stood for, booze etc, and I certainly wouldn't ever have wanted to mark him as a centre-half on the pitch with his uncontrollable (or were they really controllable) flailing elbows.

For me though he will always remain 'Big Roy' with an equally BIG heart of Gold!

Too honest for his own good at times, I was already very aware of the bloke's top qualities and that was embedded even deeper in my mind the Monday before the newly crowned GM Vauxhall Conference champions were due to play Witton Albion in the 1992 FA Trophy final at Wembley.

"How ya getting there, pal?" he asked me.

"I'm going on the special coach the *Gazette* have hired for the day," I replied.

"You're bloody not," the big fella insisted. "You're coming with us. You've been with us all season and you're going to be with us on our big day!"

"What can I say," I responded, but as it turned out I did go on the *Gazette* bus with my then wife, Liz, but not before 'Big Roy' had furnished me with every pass possible to go where I liked once I arrived at the stadium. There was a dressing room pass, a pitch pass, pass to sit on the subs bench and a pass to go into the banqueting hall after the match.

U's chairman at the time, James Bowdidge, had also given my wife and I an invitation to watch the match as his guests from the Royal Box with other Colchester dignitaries and former players. So, after I saw Liz to her seat, coincidentally next to U's FA Cup hero and Leeds United conqueror Dave Simmons, a former neighbour of ours, I wandered down to the dressing room area where I joined Roy and the players as they strolled out onto the pitch to soak up the atmosphere.

The U's fans were in good voice, all 24,000 of them in a crowd of almost 28,000 and then we all strolled back into the dressing room to prepare for the match. U's coach Ian 'Skip' Phillips delivered the pre-match team talk and then it was time to walk out again for the big kick-off.

The crescendo of noise that hit our ears as we emerged from the tunnel behind Roy and the team was deafening and I thought to myself, *what on earth must it sound like with 100,000 fans in here?* The U's supporters were singing all the way as we walked round the track surrounding the pitch to the subs benches from where I wrote my match notes. The banter passing between the two benches, sometimes bad tempered, went on throughout the match, especially when the U's dominance became apparent.

And it only took the boys five minutes to find the net via a great header from Mike 'The Big Yank' Masters who became the first American to score in a major Wembley final. Nicky Smith angered the Witton subs bench even more when he netted the U's second and, as the volley of abuse became even louder, Mike Lutkevitch scored to haul the Cheshire club back into the contest.

The nerve-ends became frayed even further when referee Kieron Barratt, who had let the Witton players get away with murder, sent-off U's midfielder Jason Cook for violent conduct with nine minutes still to play after he squared-up to his marker following yet another rough tackle. Enter the silky-skilled Steve McGavin to make the game safe with a typical match-winner in the 89th minute as the blue and white ribbons were already being tied to the resplendent trophy.

I'll never forget that wonderful sight of U's skipper Tony English climbing the Wembley steps to hold the magnificent piece of silverware aloft – a sight I never thought I would ever see a Colchester captain do in my lifetime – and I'll never forget the superb gesture of unused sub Eamonn Collins handing Jason Cook his winner's medal that the stingy rule-book crazy FA had refused to present to him.

Suddenly, it was all over after the on-field celebrations and photos and it was back into the dressing rooms for even more fun and games.

As 'The Big Yank' proudly showed off his winner's medal I was photographed by my *Gazette* colleague Steve Argent with the trophy lid on my head, but I had to leave the boys to enjoy the rest of their night as I was rushed back to the *Gazette* office to write up my match report and all the triumphant quotes that went with it for the eight-page FA Trophy special that hit the streets the next day. What a day. A day that will live in my memory forever thanks to 'Big Roy.'

Little did I know it then, but I was to go back to Wembley twice more in the next six years to watch the U's in finals again. The first of those two big money-spinning outings to the twin towers came on Sunday afternoon, 20 April 1997, when the U's met Carlisle United in the Auto Windscreens Shield final. Manager Steve Wignall proved as generous as McDonough and invited me to travel to Wembley with the players.

We stayed overnight in a posh Hertfordshire hotel, the same hotel as north London giants Arsenal used for their pre-match get together. The Gunners were due to play Blackburn Rovers at home on the same day. All their big names were there and a we enjoyed a long chat with their managerial duo Arsene Wenger and his assistant Pat Rice. Wenger even autographed a U's shirt for me.

The U's fans were out in force again and as we made our way to Wembley, it seemed as though the whole town of Colchester were making the trip with us. There were blue and white colours everywhere as we made the journey along Wembley Way and a fabulous crowd of over 45,000 greeted the players as they entered the field of play.

I was in the official Wembley press box for this one and included in the Carlisle party that day were future U's players Warren Aspinall and Stephane Pounewatchy, plus manager Mick Wadsworth. I vividly recall the sound of M People lead singer Heather Small belting out the lyrics of 'Search For The Hero Inside Yourself' before the two, well-matched teams fought out a tense goalless draw.

The final was eventually decided in the Cumbrians' favour after U's skipper Peter Cawley and teenager Karl Duguid both missed their spot-kicks in the penalty shoot-out.

My lasting memory of that day was the distraught and inconsolable Duguid shedding floods of tears because he felt he had let the team down. Little more than twelve months later, young Duguid had the chance to put matters right as the U's earned the right to play Torquay United in the Division Three Play-off final on Friday night, 22 May 1998. The final was switched to Friday because England were due to play Saudi Arabia in a meaningless friendly the following day.

Once again, Wiggy did me the honours and we stayed at the same hotel and travelled to Wembley with a group of police outriders escorting our team coach through the red traffic lights and heavy Friday night traffic. As we made our way, I remember thinking, *if I was travelling home from work that's all I would want, a bunch of bloody footballers making me late.*

Torquay included former U's favourite Paul Gibbs in their line-up and another tense match resulted in a David Gregory 22nd minute winner from the penalty spot, while U's keeper Carl Emberson earned the Man of the Match plaudits with a string of super saves to keep The Gulls at bay.

Young Duguid's beaming smile said it all as U's captain Richard Wilkins climbed the famous thirty-nine steps to hoist the impressive Play-Off Trophy aloft to the sound of the triumphant U's army of fans belting out 'We're going up – we're going up – the U's are going up!'

Then it was back to that by now well-worn routine in the *Gazette* office to write another eight-page cup-winning special. I really was getting used to it all by now thanks to 'Big Roy' and Wiggy.

Thanks for so many wonderful memories guys!

CHAPTER 11
I WAS THERE

How many times have you heard someone say, "I was there," when something magical, historical or simply amazing grabbed the attention of the whole nation?

Well, as I've already pointed out earlier in this book I was there for Colchester United's three Wembley finals; I was there to see the U's win the GM Vauxhall Conference Championship and promotion back into the Football League and I was down at Yeovil to see Phil Parkinson's squad clinch a historic promotion up into the Championship – the highest position the tiny Essex minnows have ever achieved in their near eighty-year history.

I was also there on a rain-lashed, windswept Saturday afternoon in late September 1991 when U's goalkeeper Scott Barrett created a new chapter of U's history by stunning the 5,186 crowd with a bizarre last minute winner against Conference title rivals Wycombe Wanderers at Adams Park.

It was simply unbelievably amazing! The scores were locked at 1-1 as the hard-fought, highly charged encounter raced into the final sixty seconds when 'The Goalie' – as Barrett was known to his team-mates – unleashed a fantastic, last-gasp, long-range missile from inside his own penalty area which was carried by the gale-force wind deep into the Wanderers territory where it skidded off the rain-soaked turf over the head of startled Wycombe keeper Paul Hyde into the empty net. The home fans couldn't believe what they had just witnessed and, to be honest, neither could everyone connected with Col U.

I don't think 'The Goalie' himself could believe what he had just done. His amazing strike wasn't just a perfect U's winner, it was also the first time a Colchester United keeper had scored in open play in the club's illustrious history and it left the angry 'Chairboys' boss Martin O'Neill spitting feathers.

Arms raised to the heavens in triumph, Barrett was immediately engulfed by his ecstatic team-mates and, as he faced the media soon after the game, he modestly pointed out, "It was just one of those things, but it couldn't have happened at a better time, or in a more important game. The goal won us three valuable points against a dangerous Wycombe side that went into the match sitting proudly at the top of the table.

"You never guess things like this are going to happen and I came away feeling sorry for Nicky Smith, who had just scored his first goal for the club. He told me I'd stolen his thunder!"

Unbelievably, the former Notts County, Wolves and Stoke City keeper had achieved a similar feat much earlier in his colourful career when finding the net in a Central Midland League game as an eighteen-year-old.

"I'm going for my hat-trick now," he jokingly said.

His all-important winner at Wycombe was to prove vital as the U's went on to do the double over their Buckinghamshire rivals – winning the home match 3-0 with a Steve McGavin brace and one from Gary Bennett – before going on to pip their rivals to the title and promotion by virtue of a better goal-difference after both sides finished the season level on 94 points.

I was also there in 1959 as a thirteen-year-old to watch Colchester come from 2-0 down to force a draw against mighty Arsenal – then the top side in the country – with goals from John Evans and Neil Langman in a fourth round FA Cup tie. I was there at Highbury four nights later when the U's crashed out of the cup 4-0 in the frosty, fog-bound replay before a bumper crowd of almost 63,000. Sadly, I never got into the ground for this one as they locked the gates with me and my dad just two yards away.

I was there two years later when two goals from Martyn King, plus one apiece from Tommy Williams and Peter Wright humbled north-east giants Newcastle United 4-1 in a Layer Road, first round League Cup-tie in which tiny Scottish wizard of dribble Sammy McLeod ran the visitors ragged.

I was there in January 1968 when the referee denied the U's a winner for an alleged handball in a 1-1 FA Cup third round draw against West Bromwich Albion. I was there again for the replay at the Hawthorns four days later as the U's crashed out 4-0 before a crowd of over 40,000.

I was there for the fantastic, historic FA Cup fifth round win over mighty Leeds United and I was at Goodison Park three weeks later as Dick Graham's brave Division Four battlers lost 5-0 against Everton in front of a bumper crowd of almost 54,000.

I was there for the FA Cup fourth round clash with Derby County in 1977 when the referee inflamed the visitors by adding on an extra five minutes for their time wasting. U's goal-getter Colin Garwood punished the visitors further by netting the 1-1 equaliser in the dying seconds which led to nasty scenes of disappointment from the Derby fans as they left the ground. They won the replay 1-0 four days later.

I was there again in February 1979 to see Manchester United scrape into a sixth round FA Cup match thanks to a dying minutes' Jimmy Greenhoff winner in a Layer Road fifth round tie.

I was at Stamford Bridge to see Phil Parkinson's U's put up a brave fight before bowing out of the FA Cup to Jose Mourinho's Chelsea 3-1 in 2006 and, more recently, I was there to see the U's battle hard before losing at home 4-1 to in-form Tottenham Hotspur in February this year.

CHAPTER 12
SHEARER AND GAZZA CALLING

I had given up on Alan Shearer and Paul 'Gazza' Gascoigne contacting me.

I had faxed the pair of them two weeks earlier at their respective clubs, Blackburn Rovers and Glasgow Rangers, to wish U's injured ace Steve Whitton well and offer valuable advice on how to recover from a career-threatening cruciate ligament injury and get playing again.

Why should I have worried, for on the afternoon of Tuesday, 4 October 1995, three weeks after Whitts suffered his horrendous injury, the telephone rang and my *Gazette* colleague, Julie Lay, said, "It's Alan Shearer for you."

"Pull the other one," I said, "He won't be phoning me now." But she assured me it was Alan and, sure as hell, it was him.

"You've got as long as it takes my young daughter, who's asleep on my lap, to wake up," said the popular England international striker, "What do you want to know?"

I told him about Whitts' injury and asked him what pitfalls and setbacks could he endure in his fight to get back. Shearer, Gascoigne and former U's boss, ex-Ipswich Town favourite, George Burley, were three international stars who had made full recoveries from their particular cruciate injuries.

"First of all, Steve must stay positive," said Alan.

"There will be many times when he will feel very frustrated, times when he feels life is getting on top of him, but I can assure him things will gradually get better and better. When he's had the operation it's ups all the way from there."

Nursed back to full fitness by the delicate skills of Cambridge surgeon David Dandy – one of the country's top injury specialists and the man who will be operating on Whitton – Shearer claimed he was now as good as he ever was.

"Even at thirty-four-years-old, if Steve is in good shape and a positive thinker, I can't see any reason why his age should be against him. Once the soreness of the first two weeks is out of the way he will begin to feel that he is moving forward again.

"My advice to him is not to be too ambitious in setting himself comeback targets and to retain a sense of humour through the worst of times. If he doesn't attempt to hurry things everything will be all right.

"Steve will suffer a lot of downs and disappointments along the way. He will have to put them to the back of his mind and get over the tough times in the best way he can.

"Whenever I felt down, I played with my kids and when I began to feel really down I escaped to the Seychelles with my wife. A couple of weeks in the sun worked wonders for me.

"As long as he is prepared to be patient and not overdo things I'm sure Steve will make a full recovery – I wish him well."

It took Gazza another couple of weeks to hit my base and when he did, once again, I told Julie Lay to, "Piss off, you're having me on."

"It really is him," Julie insisted, thrusting the phone in my direction and, would you believe it, the multi-million pound Rangers and England star promptly sent

Whitts a 'You can make it' message.

Speaking to me en-route to Rangers European Cup-tie against Juventus in Turin, Gazza said: "If Steve's got the will to fight back he will make it. Age means nothing if you've looked after yourself."

Whitts had already confessed to being flattered by the support of Alan Shearer, but he said he was almost rendered speechless when he learned Gazza too had weighed in with words of wisdom for his battle to play League football again.

"The Colchester lads will absolutely slaughter me for this," he said, "But I'm completely bowled over to think two stars like Gazza and Alan Shearer have taken time out to support me."

Gazza pointed out, "I was ready to play again nine months after snapping my cruciate ligament in the 1991 FA Cup final and if Steve doesn't overdo things he'll be flying again in four to five months' time.

"If I was him now I would resign myself to a reasonable break, as I did, and tell himself I am going to get back!

"Steve's going to experience a lot of pain and boredom first and he's simply got to fight his way through it.

"He'll suffer a great deal of swelling around the knee for some time yet, but once he gets his leg working properly again he will soon feel he's moving in the right direction.

"The fact that Steve is thinking about becoming a manager will certainly help him while he's out of action. He'll have a good chance to find out what being a manager is all about."

CHAPTER 13
IAN RUSH(ES) TO HAIL GERAINT

Steve Whitton is not the only U's player to receive backing from a top international star.

His good friend and former Layer Road team-mate, Geraint 'George' Williams, had a goodwill message from fellow Welsh international Ian Rush when he was handed the Colchester manager's job in November 2006.

The legendary ex-Liverpool and Juventus striker exclusively told me at the *Gazette*, "I'm not at all surprised to see Geraint doing so well. Colchester United may have unearthed a great manager.

"He has always been a hard worker and he was a good organiser when we were international team-mates. Geraint is clearly cut out to be a coach or manager. What he has achieved in taking Colchester to a higher level following the departure of Phil Parkinson is simply phenomenal.

"It just goes to show the kind of input he must have had as coach to Phil Parkinson in Colchester's promotion-winning season."

Rush added: "One of the hardest things in football is to be a coach or a manager. Geraint lives his life for football and we enjoyed a good time working together.

"He was always the first one there and the last one away and his coaching skills were of a high quality. He is a lovely man who is now getting the rewards for his coaching and managerial ability.

"To do what he has done with a small club like Colchester is a tremendous achievement. I'm so pleased for him."

Williams won thirteen international caps as a midfielder with Wales during the 1980s and 1990s, nine of them in the same line-up as renowned goal-poacher Rush, who went on to wear the blood-red Dragons jersey seventy-three times.

He won almost every honour in the game in a playing career spanning from 1979-2000 and he also pointed out that he and Williams enjoyed two years together studying for their Pro Coaching licence at Aberystwyth and Cardiff.

Rush added, "I played international football with some great guys like Mark Hughes (now managing Stoke City) and Chris Coleman (the current Wales senior manager).

"Both of them went on to become Premier League managers with Blackburn Rovers and Fulham respectively. I see no reason why Geraint cannot follow in their footsteps."

Williams is currently manager of the national Wales Under-21 squad.

CHAPTER 14
SUFFERING THE PAIN

Snow, ice and absolutely no football.

The winter of 1990-91 really took its toll on our national sport and, in Colchester United's case, it wiped out all the GM Vauxhall Conference action for the freezing month of February. That said, player-manager Ian Atkins still had to keep his players fit and, in my case, I still had to find some stories.

The local sports scene was hit equally as hard with no junior football, rugby or hockey to fall back on so I had to put the Ponder thinking cap on and come up with the odd feature or two.

I know, I thought to myself, *why don't I ask Ackers if I can join him and the U's players in the gym?* I wasn't too many weeks away from celebrating my 47th birthday but I thought, *there's still life in this old dog yet.*

Furthermore, professional footballers get their money for nothing don't they!

I knew I was out of shape and overweight but I said to myself, *they won't be going at it too hard and training will be an absolute doddle* – how wrong can one silly old sod be!

The grey haired Ponder bulk didn't know what it was letting itself in for when Ackers slung a set of training kit my way and said, "Get your fat arse in here and join in."

Thank God physio Brian Owen was on hand to keep things in check and he whispered in my ear, "Don't try to prove anything, Frannie, just do what you can. Nobody's expecting you to keep up with the lads.

"You will come in for a bit of ribbing 'cos that's the nature of the game, but the lads will think all the more of you 'cos you're ready to give it a go."

Brian's assurances made me feel so much better, but then I was reminded that training keeps the limbs and muscles loose and the mind sharp.

"We'll build you legs of iron and stomach muscles of steel," he said. Well, I don't know what went wrong in my case because what they didn't tell me was the legs would be iron jelly and the stomach an agonised contorted mess.

Thankfully, I missed the warm-up run but, as I eagerly slipped into my shirt, shorts and socks, memories of those long ago Scraley Road training nights – under the watchful eye of Heybridge Swifts' tough task master Gordon Haggerty – suddenly came flooding back.

Dear old Gordon was an angel compared to BO, U's goalkeeper Scott Barrett and Steve 'Zorro' Foley, the men in charge of training that day. They kept us hard at it with little respite and word had it this terrible trio had escaped from the Hammer House of Horrors that very day.

I should have realised what I was letting myself in for the moment I saw Ackers, Neale Marmon, Scott Daniels and Shaun Elliott sweating bucket loads in BO's bench sessions.

"Get stuck in, Frannie," said BO, "And remember, I want your touch to be as light as a feather."

I've never been renowned for my light touch, poise or balance. When this old body gets moving there's only one way to stop as midfield genius Eamonn Collins found to his cost when my left knee thundered into his back.

"I think you'd better sit this one out," said Brian, and that was my cue to go and join Scotty Barrett's floor sessions.

Tucked in alongside 'Big Roy,' Mario 'The Lizard' Walsh and Mark 'Horses' Yates we quickly slipped through a few row-boats and cycling routines. Just when the poor old stomach muscles were beginning to feel the strain, ring-master Barrett cracked his whip to send the pain and agony of sit-ups and press-ups through my aching limbs again.

I was practically down and out by now, but there was still 'Zorro's five-a-side game to come. After watching Eamonn, Mark 'Sheedy' Kinsella and Nicky 'Smudger' Smith in action my skills as a goal poacher – in place of McDonough – were quickly put to the test when Mark Radford set me up in front of an empty net.

Any thoughts I had of capping my day with a goal rapidly evaporated, however. The chance had fallen to my left foot and that's the one I can only stand on. My performance was cruelly likened to that of the famous old Fable – The Hare and the Tortoise – only in my case the tortoise didn't win.

Suddenly, it was all over. The sweat and the torture were easily outweighed by the fun and enjoyment and, the camaraderie within the camp.

As for me? "You won't even make the youth team with hair that colour," quipped Foley, but make no bones about it – anyone who tells you footballers don't earn their money should try it for themselves, as I did.

I still had my moments even though I was totally knackered and my lasting memory of the day was nutmegging little Irish wizard Collins with my first touch of the ball. He's been going round knock-kneed ever since.

Thanks for putting up with this unfit old hack, lads!

CHAPTER 15
BURLEY BATTLE

It was a frost-bound, freezing Friday night on 16 December 1994 when I said goodnight to Colchester United manager George Burley for the last time.

We had just witnessed his U's battlers climb into the fringes of the Division Three play-off spots for the first time in the 1994-95 season with a great 2-1 win at Doncaster Rovers thanks to a 20-yard sizzler from big Pete Cawley and another goal from busy striker Steve Brown.

Little did I know it then, but it was the last time I was to see Burley, who on Christmas Eve decided to walk-out on the Layer Road club only six months into his two-year contract to manage the team he had represented so magnificently as a player – the U's East Anglian rivals, Ipswich Town.

Fans of the U's were totally unaware of Burley's shock move until they turned up for the Boxing Day morning clash with Northampton Town at which time rumours began to circulate around the ground that the manager had, in fact, departed. So began, what became known as, the long running Burley Saga!

The U's had only months earlier stunned the Layer Road fans by naming the ex-Ayr United boss as their new manager, a move which caught the entire Anglian media circus by surprise.

It began to look like a catastrophic appointment when their shock choice of team boss couldn't conjure-up a win for love nor money in his first half-a-dozen matches. However, once he got started, Burley and his squad embarked on a tremendous run of 21 League and cup outings with only three defeats, which left the U's handily placed in the race for play-off places. I am confident that, had he stayed at Layer Road, the U's would have gone on to win promotion – maybe even as Third Division champions!

Sadly, everything went pear-shaped after Christmas. All the bitter wrangling between the U's and Ipswich Town hierarchy began to take over from the football and Colchester eventually finished, what had been a very promising season, in tenth place.

The boardroom battle and compensation wrangle had been raging ever since; for a staggering 922 days – almost three years – before the unsavoury situation came to a head and the problem was finally resolved by an FA tribunal in London.

The two clubs were informed that the tribunal's decision would be binding – which they both accepted. There was to be no appeals procedure and speculation involving compensation sums of between £50,000 and £600,000 were rumoured to be on the table at the time. An earlier Football Association tribunal had already ordered the Suffolk club to pay Colchester £135,000, plus interest, after the clubs had met head-on in a two-day case in the City to finally sort out the matter.

"We feel we have been totally vindicated in our stance concerning the George Burley case and we are delighted with the outcome," said U's chairman Gordon Parker.

It is understood the U's pocketed a total pay-out of between £250,000 and £300,000 from the case following tribunal chairman Timothy Charlton QC's ruling.

However, a large amount of that pay-out would be eaten up by the U's barristers' fees, while Ipswich Town had to fork out another £50,000 on their own court costs.

CHAPTER 16
ON MY FA YOUTH CUP TRAVELS

Colchester United youth team bosses, Steve Foley and Micky Cook, did me the great honour of being allowed to travel with the U's kids in their quest for FA Youth Cup glory.

It might not at the time have been seen as glory by many onlookers but for a little club such as Colchester to reach the last sixteen of the top youth competition in the country – as they did against mighty Aston Villa on Monday, 30 January 1995 – was no mean feat at all.

Steve invited me to join the boys on the team coach to Villa Park – what a fantastic stadium that is – where they came up against a Villa side that had lost just one of their last nineteen outings.

Plucky U's eventually crashed out 4-0 but, for the majority of the match, spectators could have been forgiven for wondering just which of the two teams doing battle out there on the pitch was the Premier League side. Steve summed up the difference perfectly after the match when he said: "If you don't put away your chances you don't win matches!"

The Young U's created at least twelve good chances and enjoyed the lion's share of the play in the opening half. With that kind of good fortune, Villa, twice winners already of the prestigious trophy, should have been looking forward to having their name engraved on the cup again in a further three months' time. That honour, however, went to Manchester United, who beat Tottenham Hotspur 4-3 on penalties after the two sides had finished the two legged final all square at 2-2 after extra time. Future U's first teamer Simon Brown played in goal for Spurs at the time.

Anyway, back to the young U's and Aston Villa, who were coached by Villa Park legend Peter Withe and watched by first team manager, Brian Little. The Villa kids looked anything but Premier League pedigree as Foley's boys took the game to them, but once the home team went ahead the writing was on the wall.

Villa's goals came via Lee Hendrie, a future first team star, Lee Burchell, Darren Byfield and late substitute Richard Burgess. Defeated U's may have been – disgraced never!

Foley's boys did the town proud and to think only three months earlier that same Villa Park pitch was gracing Italy's Inter Milan in UEFA Champions League action.

Funnily enough my own long standing memory of that match was the carpeting – sporting the Aston Villa club crest – from the front entrance, through the dressing rooms, almost to the touchline out on to the pitch.

Steve Foley later that year let me enjoy inside knowledge of the young U's Southern Junior Floodlit Cup first round tie against West Ham United at Layer Road. The U's put on another great display before going down 2-1 to a young Hammers side that included future England internationals Frank Lampard and Rio Ferdinand, plus future U's first team star, left-back Joe Keith.

My next sojourn into FA Youth Cup action was a two legged, fourth round tie against mighty Blackburn Rovers youngsters on Tuesday night 25 January 2001. Micky Cook's kids forced a splendid 2-2 draw in that first match at Rovers magnificent Ewood Park stadium, hitting back from 2-0 down to draw level with two superb Lloyd Opara goals – the first one a brilliant 30-yard chip after spotting home keeper Ryan Robinson well off his line.

I vividly recall writing my match report sitting in the Ewood Park directors' box and Graeme Souness, Rovers first team boss at the time, leaning over my shoulder and saying, "That's a great little team you've got there."

Earlier in the day, Cook's boys and I had enjoyed all the lavish treatment of travel on the classy first team coach and pre-match meal at a posh hotel. Micky also invited me to listen to his team-talk at the hotel and I thought to myself, *you lucky little sods. I hope you all realise the wonderful opportunity you've got to carve out a great career for yourselves.*

Sadly Cook's boys were soundly beaten in the Layer Road replay and Blackburn went on to meet Arsenal in the final where they were beaten 6-3.

Phil Parkinson's U's League One promotion winning side in 2006 included Neil Danns, who starred for Blackburn in those two FA Youth Cup-ties, along with current Stoke City and Republic of Ireland international striker, Jon Walters.

The best was yet to come for me though, when Micky Cook asked me to join him, coach Adrian Webster and the boys for a third round FA Youth Cup-tie against the mighty Arsenal at Highbury – marble halls and all – on Tuesday, 3 December 2002. What an experience for the lads to be playing at that legendary north London stadium and I'll never forget walking through the main entrance, through the corridor from the dressing rooms out to the centre of the pitch with the giant grandstands swallowing me up from all sides.

Micky said: "It's the ultimate game you hope to have every year when you're pitched against the best of the best – and every one of my boys is up for it. They've been handed the chance to play against one of the biggest clubs in one of the best stadiums in the country.

"It's another big part of a tremendous learning curve and I will be urging my boys to go out and enjoy themselves. I will be reminding them of our club's great cup tradition and the fact that they are playing against the youth team of the reigning Premier League champions."

As things turned out the game ended in another success for the Premier League Academy over the Football League's Scholarship. Cook's young Layer Road starlets were undone by goals early in each half and the crestfallen U's boss summed up his feelings by saying, "To get a positive result at places like Highbury we needed a few five-star performances and our keeper Dean Gerken aside, we didn't get any."

The Arsenal line-up boasted eight youth internationals, while the U's fielded Gerken, fullback John White and midfielder Greg Halford, who have all gone on to enjoy lucrative Football League careers.

Gerken's outstanding display was highly praised by Youth International goalkeeper coach Ray Clemence, the former Liverpool, Spurs and England star, who was running his eye over several of the young Gunners players.

Great times and a wonderful experience. I can't thank Steve Foley, Micky Cook and Adrian Webster enough for their generosity in allowing me to be part of it.

CHAPTER 17
GOODBYE OLD FRIENDS

It's always sad when old friends are forced to bring down the curtain on their career with a lot of mileage still left in the tank. Three such examples of that came in the premature eclipse of Colchester United captains Tony English, Richard Wilkins and Simon Clark.

English, the longest serving player at Layer Road at the time, was only twenty-nine-years-old when he was forced to quit just ten days before the start of the new 1996-97 season after failing to recover from a knee operation two-and-a-half-months earlier.

Commonly known by his nickname 'Squid', English, one of two brothers to play for the U's, made 513 league and cup appearances for the club between 1985-96, scoring fifty-nine goals. The seven-times capped England Youth international played in every position for the U's, including goalkeeper, but was generally regarded as a midfielder or defender.

Clearly upset at having to call it a day because of injury, after a U's career spanning twelve years, English told me, "The injury went back as far as 1993 and I am no longer prepared to pack my body with pain-killers to get myself through day-to day-training.

"I could have gone on with the use of cortisone injections in the knee to kill the pain, but I wasn't prepared to risk the threat of being in a wheelchair later in life because of the increasing damage I might have done to myself."

The popular club captain, who only four years earlier enjoyed the greatest day of his footballing life when hoisting aloft the FA Trophy at Wembley, exactly a week after skippering the U's back into the Football League as GM Vauxhall Conference champions, went on, "I want to bow out of the game with the fans remembering me for the player I was. The club has been fantastic about it and obviously I'm bitterly disappointed that my career should have been ended this way. I'm going to miss playing for Colchester United because I've enjoyed every minute of it, but maybe I can come back one day – maybe as manager."

Signing off for the last time, English said he will always be best remembered for his favourite saying, "I captained the U's out of the League and I captained them back in again!"

What a fitting finale.

It was a similar story for the unlucky Wilkins when the final whistle was sounded prematurely on his U's career at the age of thirty-four-years-old with just eight games left to play of the 1999-2000 season. Like Tony English, Richard Wilkins was not only an inspirational captain, he was also a great Colchester United ambassador. Wilkins was forced to quit in late March having been advised to retire after seeing a specialist about a serious neck injury following the U's 2-1 win at Oldham Athletic the previous November.

"It was a massive blow to me because, in my heart of hearts, I wanted the specialist to tell me that I could carry on playing," said the stylish midfielder or defender.

He added: "It's very difficult to come to terms with and obviously I'm disappointed it's had to end this way. I confess it won't be easy knowing that I won't ever be involved in Football League or cup action again. When football has been your life, decisions like this are hard to swallow. It would have been nice to have carried on playing, but my long-term health is more important.

"I know it's the right thing to do because I'm still suffering a lot of pain, but I have enjoyed a great four years back at the club and I know it's better for me to go out with the fans remembering me for being a good player rather than an old wreck only able to play the occasional game."

The very popular Wilkins said, "At least I went out on a high note in my final game in front of our home fans, playing against Burnley's former England international striker Ian Wright. I will always remember as well, lifting the Division Three Promotion Play-Off Cup at Wembley Stadium two years earlier."

Wilkins made a total of 305 League and cup appearances for the U's in two spells at the club between 1996 to 2000. He initially signed from Haverhill Rovers in 1996 before joining Cambridge United for £65,000 following the U's relegation out of the League in 1990.He joined Hereford United on a free transfer in 1994 before being snapped up again by U's boss Steve Wignall two years later for £30,000.

Simon Clark made only sixty-four League and cup appearances for the U's before his shock departure for 'personal reasons' at the end of the 2001-02 season. Signed from Leyton Orient as the club's new skipper before the start of the 2000-01 season, the truth of the matter is the thirty-four-year-old central defender was never the same player following a fatal car crash in Colchester town centre in which a pedestrian died in a collision with his Ford Mondeo.

In a horror story *Gazette* exclusive seventeen days later, Clark, speaking for the first time about the tragic accident, told me, "The whole thing has been an absolute nightmare. I sincerely regret everything that has happened, but my therapist has encouraged me to talk openly about the accident."

Badly shaken by the incident, which happened at the traffic lights at the top of Balkerne Hill, Clark said: "It fazed me a bit when I had to stop at the lights again. They turned red and my mind and my eyes were everywhere just waiting for something to happen again."

CHAPTER 18
RULES ARE THERE TO BE BROKEN

There's a golden rule in journalism; never to give an interviewee an opportunity to change his or her story. Well I committed the cardinal sin by doing exactly that and if my editor had found out, there's no doubt I would have been sacked.

In my defence, I still maintain my decision paid dividends because the great stories I gained in future times, along with the trust and further tip-offs, more than made-up for the sizzling scoop I missed out on.

I committed my sin on Saturday morning, 9 April 1991 with the U's well on the way to achieving promotion from the GM Vauxhall Conference back into the Football League at the first time of asking. A win at struggling Northwich Victoria's historic Drill Field ground would have taken the U's to the top of the table for the first time in the season with only seven games to play.

The Essex visitors were coasting at 2-1 ahead with only thirty seconds to play when their one-time England B international, Shaun Elliott, committed an even greater sin than me. Victoria's Tony Hemmings was heading away from goal and going nowhere fast when Elliott committed the schoolboy error of needlessly chopping him down in the penalty area to gift the Cheshire hosts a dramatic last gasp equaliser from the spot.

To make matters worse, former Sunderland and Norwich defender Elliott had already been guilty of making the poor clearance that handed Northwich their first equaliser just two minutes before half-time. To make matters even more worse, the U's had been ordered to pay Elliott's parent club Blackpool £7,000 for his transfer only two days earlier. Distraught U's player-boss Ian Atkins was seething blue murder when I grabbed him outside the dressing room after the match.

"He'll never kick another f**king ball for me again," Atkins choked, amid a barrage of expletives.

And some of the things he accused Elliott of afterwards were almost unrepeatable and would most definitely have landed him in court – at the very least facing a hefty suspension and/or fine from the football authorities.

"Bloody hell, Ian, do you really mean it?" I asked.

"Of course I do," he thundered. "Go ahead and print it. That needless f**king penalty may have just cost us promotion and the championship."

Christ alive, I thought to myself, *I've got a real earth shattering exclusive here*, but after sleeping on it,

I decided to give Ian a chance to confirm or change his story by phoning him the next morning.

"Bloody hell," came the voice back down the phone line. "I must have been in a real state to have said all those things. There's no way I can let you go ahead with it."

We watered the whole thing down between us although Ackers still lambasted Elliott enough to make him squirm the next time the two came face to face.

"I don't know what Elliott was thinking," the still shell-shocked U's chief went on. "Shaun had a nightmare match and I was very disappointed that a player of his experience and ability should have made such a rash challenge to give away the penalty. He must have had a sudden rush of blood to the head because the Northwich player was going nowhere when Shaun hauled him down."

Elliott's decision was to prove fatal because the U's

finished the season as runners-up to new champions Barnet by the margin of only two points.

Steve Whitton didn't want me to publish a back page splash about Lomana Tresor Lua Lua after the U's whiz-kid told me he was 'ready to dance all the way to the Premiership' following a scintillating display at Bristol Rovers. I didn't change my mind on this one! Man of the Match Lua Lua had the Rovers fans purring with amazement at his dazzling super skills despite only entering the fray after the half-time interval.

"Where do you get all those rhythmic quicksilver moves from?" I asked him.

"It's the African music I used to dance to as a kid around the campfire back home in the Democratic Republic of Congo," he said. "It all comes so naturally to me," he added, gyrating his hips and swaying rhythmically back and forth in an impromptu demonstration of the magical touches that were making him a big target for a host of top Premiership clubs.

He said: "I believe to be a good dribbler a player must have rhythm and good balance. Our music and dance around the campfire in my early days back home in Africa have given me that and now I must learn more about football and begin to know how far in this game I can go."

Whitton felt my interview would come across as a native boy in the jungle doing a war dance round the campfire. The *Gazette* printed the story!

Lua Lua lived up to his promise – he did dance all the way to the Premier League with North East giants Newcastle United.

CHAPTER 19
WAS ROGER WHO THE WORST?

There is always plenty of speculation among a football club's fans as to who were the best and worst managers to have represented their team. Colchester United is no different. The outcome does, of course, depend on the age of the supporters in question as we usually judge such things by the managers we have seen.

Former Portsmouth goalkeeper Jimmy Allen did a great job when initially guiding the U's into the Football League's old Division Three South back in 1950-51.

Ex-Arsenal and Leicester City defender Jack Butler followed next, but the first U's boss I personally remember was former Charlton Athletic hardman Benny Fenton, younger brother of the famous Ted Fenton, who guided humble little Southern League Colchester into the FA Cup fifth round as player-manager before moving on to manage West Ham. Benny did a great job, taking the U's to the brink of the original Second Division (today's Championship), missing out to Ipswich and Torquay by a solitary point.

I can go on and on, but this isn't a story about who I think are the best managers, it's more about who I think was the worst during my days as a football writer with the *Evening Gazette*. I don't have to look too hard to come up with a list of two. They are Roger Brown and Mick Wadsworth – although there have been one or two more prime candidates since then!

If you ask me to select the worst I would have to say Roger Brown.

Mike Walker, Manager of the Month for October 1987,

was unceremoniously sacked by U's chairman Jonathan Crisp when his team was riding high on top of the former Division Four (today's League Two). Walker was unbelievably replaced by the unknown Roger Who? manager of lowly non-league club Poole Town, presumably on the advice of double-winning Arsenal boss Bertie Mee, who, along with Crisp, felt that good football alone would not win the U's promotion.

How wrong could they have been?

Former Bournemouth, Norwich and Fulham centre-half Brown started his reign well by snapping up the November Manager of the Month award but, sadly, things went rapidly downhill from there as he gradually unravelled all the good things put in place by Walker with a number of dubious player and coaching signings.

Crisp told the *Gazette*: "Roger Brown has come to us highly recommended. He was a manager in industry before he started in professional football at a late age. He has proven management skills outside the game. Roger is a strong, tough, hard man and I'm sure he will do a good job for us."

What a load of old bunkum – how wrong could anyone be?

It wasn't for the lack of trying. Poor old Roger tried extremely hard, but had absolutely no idea how to manage a Football League club.

I had many an interview with Jolly Roger who, to his credit, was a very nice man, but when it came to football management he left everyone totally bamboozled. He used to tell me how after every defeat – and there were quite a few – he would drive his car to the nearest lay-by and sit there for two or three hours reliving where he and his team had gone wrong.

Sadly for Roger things never got better – only a lot

worse – and some of his ideas had to be seen to be believed. One such idea he devised for corner-kicks was an American style scrum movement where his players broke away from the would-be huddle in all directions presumably to confuse the opposition defence.

I never once saw that little scheme pay dividends.

Roger also came out with some outrageous statements, one being in mid-February 1988: "PROMOTION? Yes, but we're going up as CHAMPIONS!"

The table-topping U's side he inherited had fallen to sixth spot and, brushing aside the fact that they had gained only one point from the last 18 available, he incredibly predicted: "Promotion is ours for the taking!"

He added, "There are a lot of players with me now who I want to take up into the Second Division."

His U's had 47 points at that stage with sixteen games to play and they only managed to pick up another 20 points from the 48 available. Brown's Layer Road reign lasted just short of twelve months when he resigned three days after a humiliating club record defeat 8-0 at Leyton Orient. Sadly, he died aged fifty-eight, back in his native Tamworth in August 2011 following a long battle against cancer.

Brown was far from the worst though when you look at the club's long list of team bosses throughout their near eighty-year history.

The prize for the worst ever clearly went to Ron Meades, who lasted just four days in the job back in June 1953. Manager of the tiny, unknown north Cornwall club, Wadebridge Town, Meades claimed he had played for Cardiff City when interviewed. He was appointed U's boss ten days later only to have the offer withdrawn after some disturbing news was unearthed by the local newspaper – but not before he had signed a contract and chaired a players' meeting. His four-day stay remains the shortest managerial reign in the club's history.

Historic moment – U's captain Tony English hoists aloft the FA Trophy at Wembley

Tony English with the FA Trophy
and GM Vauxhall Conference
championship trophy

Roy McDonough proudly
shows off the Conference
trophy

The U's players celebrate their FA Trophy triumph on the Wembley pitch

If the cap fits wear it – the author with (from left) coach Steve Foley, player-manager Roy McDonough and coach Ian Phillips in the Wembley dressing room

Plenty to smile about – FA Trophy marksmen (left to right) Nicky Smith, Steve McGavin and Mike Masters, the first American to score in a Wembley final

What a difference a year makes –
Karl Duguid is all smiles as he
celebrates the U's promotion
play-off triumph at Wembley in 1998

…there was no consoling a
tearful Duguid twelve months
earlier after he missed a
spot-kick in the Auto
Windscreens Shield final penalty
shoot-out against Carlisle

U's triumphant squad celebrate with the cup after their Division Three
Promotion Play-off final success over Torquay at Wembley

U's skipper Richard Wilkins proudly hoists the Division Three
Promotion Play-off Trophy after the one-nil win over Torquay United

Manager Steve Wignall with the Division Three Promotion Play-off trophy

U's favourite Roy McDonough and the author survey the scene at Wembley

Is that you, Des?
The real Des above...

...or is that you, Des?
Francis Ponder the pretender

Dazzling left winger Peter Wright voted the *Colchester Gazette*
readers' Player of the 20th Century

Yours truly (right) surfing the radio airwaves with BBC Essex's
Colchester United commentator Neil Kelly

The U's team that forced a 2-2 FA Cup fourth round draw with mighty
Arsenal in January 1959. They lost the replay before a Highbury crowd
of 62,686. Back row (left to right): Peter Wright, Chic Milligan, Percy Ames,
Russell Blake, Neil Langman, John Evans. Front: Cyril Hammond, Derek
Parker, George Fisher (capt), Sammy McLeod, John Fowler

Scottish wizard of dribble
Sammy McLeod, one of the
U's all-time greats

Tough talking legendary Scottish
manager Jock Wallace worked
his magic with the U's

The author is put through
his paces in the gym

On the ball Frannie –
on the ball

Commercial duo John Schultz (left) and Brian Wheeler, alias Laurel
and (That's another fine mess you got me into) Hardy enjoy a spot
of Layer Road fun

Too many cooks spoil the broth as U's chefs Peter Cawley (left)
and Mark Sale found to their cost

Layer Road panto time (back row left to right): Tony Adcock, Mark Sale, Scott Stamps. (Middle): David Gregory. (Front): David Rainford, Joe Dunne

Future manager Joe Dunne cuts
a dashing figure in a mini-dress

Striker Tony Adcock was
no boa anywhere near goal

Three Wise Men (left to right) Micky Cook, Tony Adcock
and Steve Wignall show their age

Panto Dame Scott Stamps looks a real picture with his lipstick on

Posh Boys David (left) and Neil Gregory look very dapper before a game against their former club Peterborough 'The Posh' United

England international ace Alan Shearer shocked injured U's star Steve Whitton with a get well soon phone call

Steve Whitton gets right into the spirit of the occasion as he celebrates his 100th U's appearance as a centurion

Peter Cawley with his dustbin
full of trouble

England star Paul 'Gazza'
Gascoigne phoned to wish
injured Steve Whitton well

Peter Shilton, England's most capped goalkeeper, 1,000
Premiership and Football League appearances

Manchester City and Chelsea star Shaun Wright-Phillips enjoyed himself with the U's Youth Squad

Marie 'Chirpy' Partner, the First Lady of Colchester United.

U's triumphant squad celebrate their promotion to the Championship on the final day of the 2005-06 season at Yeovil

CHAPTER 20
FA CUP HORRORS

'HUMILIATION – TERRIERS SAVAGE UNITED'.

That was how I described the U's diabolical FA Cup rout at the hands of virtually unknown Bedlington Terriers.

"Bedlington who?" we all asked when the tiny Northumberland part-time minnows came out of the hat to host Steve Wignall's Football League, Second Division men in mid-November 1998.

I've witnessed some absolute horrors in my days covering Colchester United, but this easily ranks as the worst ever. To be beaten 4-1 in the first round by a team a good five divisions lower in football's pyramid was total annihilation and embarrassment and, furthermore, we had to travel almost the length of the country to suffer it.

I knew the boys were in for a hard time when the already muddy, Terriers' Doctor Pit Welfare pitch was made even worse by heavy rain during the pre-match warm-up. Many of the same U's team had already given manager Wignall two Wembley finals, but on this day they simply weren't at the races.

"Not one individual performed in my team, while the Terriers players lived up to their name and all played stormers," groaned a deeply disappointed and humiliated U's boss. "While we slipped and slid around they chased everything down and, credit to them, they won with total endeavour. There's an old saying that you're only as good as your last match and right now we are the mugs.

"To be beaten one-nil by non-league opposition is just about bearable, but to be beaten four-one is a major embarrassment," choked the red-faced, visibly shaken, U's boss.

Twice before in Wignall's reign his team had come unstuck against non-league opposition, but they in no way were expecting what was about to be hurled at them.

The reigning Arnott Insurance Northern League Division One champions were about to celebrate the eve of their half-centenary with a perfect fairy tale result. They snapped around the ankles of the shell-shocked U's players like tireless and mischievous puppies and on a cramped, sticky and undulated pitch they set about creating the greatest chapter in their FA Cup history.

Undefeated at home in their league and cups since the previous February, Bedlington didn't have to wait too long before they hit the goal trail again. Disaster struck for the Essex visitors when Terriers' central defender Tommy Ditchburn glanced a Martin Pike free-kick past U's keeper Carl Emberson with only sixteen minutes gone. The roof was lifted off the tin-shack stand again just seven minutes later when the ball broke kindly for John Milner to side-foot number two into an empty U's net. The northern minnows pulled even further ahead when Mickey Cross floated a cross-cum-shot over Emberson's head into the net. Milner then added insult to injury when he got up from a rash Paul Buckle tackle to send Emberson the wrong way from the penalty spot with just four minutes left. Four-nil ahead and soaking up every minute of their success, Bedlington relaxed just long enough for late substitute Tony Adcock to strike for the U's with an 88th minute header.

Wignall was so incensed that he refused to dish out the

crate of booze he had brought along for the players to celebrate. Even worse, when players' spokesman Peter Cawley made his way to the front of the coach to ask if they could call in at a fish and chip shop, Wiggy replied bluntly, "No bloody chance. You lot haven't earned fish and chips. Eat the rolls, cheese and jam at the back of the bus."

The U's themselves had built an impressive record as cup giant killers over the years, but another big banana skin awaited them in November 2000 in the shape of a CATASTROPHIC CALAMITY 5-1 first round defeat at Conference leaders Yeovil.

U's boss Steve Whitton lamented, "This is the worst result of my entire career both as a player and manager and it hurts like hell. I hope my players are as hurt and embarrassed as I am."

The U's caved in alarmingly against jubilant Colin Addison's Huish Stadium squad, conceding five goals in a crazy 35-minute spell in the second half, while Karl Duguid netted the sole reply at the other end.

"The FA Cup is all about character and bottle," said a shocked and angry Whitton. "We played like eleven strangers when everything started to go wrong and while we were feeling sorry for ourselves Yeovil simply wanted it more than us!"

There was more first round woe at home to Chester in 2002 when the Conference high-fliers shocked the U's with a 2-0 defeat. It was a similar story in 1997-98 when the U's bowed out 5-4 on penalties at non-league Hereford after drawing 1-1 after extra time in a replay at Edgar Street, having already fought out a 1-1 home stalemate.

It proved even worse in 1995-96 when the U's were totally outplayed in a 2-0 defeat at Southern League minnows Gravesend and Northfleet which prompted boss Wignall to brand his players "Cowards!"

Roy McDonough described his defence as "Bloody frightening" when his U's squad scored three times but still lost 4-3 at home to Diadora League premier division outfit Sutton United in a November 1993 "KAMIKAZE CUP SHOCKER!" "Amazing – catastrophically amazing," said McDonough. "To score three goals should be enough to win any match."

Sutton were almost a spent force when two moments of suicidal madness in a drama-packed final six minutes gifted them the title as the first non-league club to beat the U's in FA Cup action at Layer Road.

CHAPTER 21
MADCAPS AND NUTTERS

Life inside professional football is made all the more colourful when madcaps and nutters act outside the box. One such madcap was the U's own captain-marvel, Peter Cawley, who landed himself deep into garbage – sorry, trouble – with some ill-considered jokes about a dustbin pitch.

The pitch in question was the former Springfield Park home of U's Division Three rivals Wigan Athletic. As he and his Layer Road team-mates prepared to take-on The Latics on their – as Peter put it – "dustbin of a pitch," his quotes in the *Gazette* had already reached the far north and the music hall jibe sadly backfired in the shape of a 2-0 defeat. It didn't help much that our story was accompanied by a great cartoon of the U's captain dressed in a blue and white striped dustbin.

Unbeknown to the U's, Latics chairman at the time, Stephen Gage – later to become Colchester's own chief executive – lived in Clacton and was only too ready to stir up the Wigan players' emotions by pinning up big Peter's quotes in both dressing rooms. Furthermore, it didn't go down too well when the out of sorts Latics first team squad lost 3-0 to a team of dustbins dressed in Colchester United shirts in a practice match. Cawley was ordered by U's chairman Gordon Parker to retract his dustbin quotes and issue a public apology to Wigan. The *Gazette* was only too willing to assist him in his quest.

As for the nutter? It had to be seen to be believed as non-league Accrington Stanley's irate team boss, John Coleman, started raining punches at all and sundry at

Layer Road as referee Phil Joslin and the two teams made their way to the players' tunnel at the end of the match.

Hot under the collar and boiling with rage at the manner of his team's 2004 FA Cup third round 2-1 replay defeat, Coleman, at the time a Liverpool primary schoolteacher, started pushing and shoving the U's stewards and police. U's chief steward Gary Tuckwell was left with a black eye in the scuffle that broke out. Stanley assistant boss Jimmy Bell also had to be restrained, but there was no holding back Coleman as he waded in with all guns blazing. Coleman, angered by a disallowed goal and ruled out appeals for a penalty, described the referee's actions as a "double whammy" for which referee Joslin banished him to the stands for the second half of the match.

Bloody hell! I said to myself, *I've never seen a football club manager act like this* and duly presented my copy to the *Gazette* editor.

"I'm not having this," the editor said, "There's no way a school teacher would act like that. What sort of example is he setting to his pupils"?

"I saw it with my own eyes," I said, "And I'd swear to it in court if I had to."

"I don't care," the editor replied and promptly ordered the news editor to rewrite my story. It was so watered-down in the end it was hardly worth using. The editor even ordered the *Gazette* photographers to furnish Coleman's solicitors with photographic evidence of the incident as he fought the Football Association in a bid to prove his innocence.

I chuckled to myself a few weeks later, however, when I was totally vindicated by the FA. They hit schoolteacher Coleman with a guilty verdict for violent conduct, a £500 fine and a two-match touchline ban, plus a further £300 fine for a second case of violent conduct in Stanley's National Conference home clash with Aldershot a few weeks before.

CHAPTER 22
STRANDED IN YORK
AND KETTERING

Of all the places for the Colchester United team coach to breakdown it had to be somewhere like York. It couldn't have happened anywhere nearer to home like Southend, Luton or Brentford – oh no, it had to be as far away as York!

The U's had earlier in the 1992 afternoon and evening of Saturday, 19 September, been undone 2-0 by the Bootham Crescent, Division Three promotion chasers, whose win took them to the top of the table. Just to compound the U's disastrous day, they clocked up another five bookings, taking their tally to nineteen in the first ten games.

Nursing our sorrows as we boarded the coach to set out on the journey home, it was suddenly realised something was drastically wrong and, pulling into a service station on the outskirts of the famous northern town our driver, Graham Layzell, said: "That's it lads, this bus isn't going anywhere tonight!"

We sat around for over an hour waiting for news as Graham frantically telephoned his bosses, George and Barry Osborne, back home in Tollesbury. They told him to sit tight with the coach and wait for their repair mechanics to bring the appropriate spares while they rang around the York bus companies in a bid to find a company that would run us home. Thank God for the service station that's all I would say, because a couple of cups of coffee and a sandwich later, we were back on the road again.

Our driver from York was absolutely brilliant. Nothing was too much trouble for him as he was directed to go here and there to drop off the U's players. Team boss Roy McDonough came round with a hat for a tip for our stand-in man and around £40-£50 better off he dropped us off safely back at Layer Road before making the journey all over again back to his York home.

Heaven only knows what time dear old Graham Layzell made it back home. I don't know whether the Osborne's mechanics were able to repair his coach, or whether he had to be towed all the way back to Tollesbury. All I know is the next time we saw him he greeted us with the same cheery smile as he always did and dished out as much cheek as he absorbed.

The U's players suffered a similar fate some fourteen years later when, on the way home from a Tuesday night 2-1 Coca-Cola Championship defeat at Coventry City, their day turned into a real nightmare as the team-coach suddenly burst into flames.

After being kept from the comfort of his bed until five o'clock the following morning, goalkeeper Aiden Davison told the *Gazette*: "Luckily, we still live to all tell the tale!"

The state-of-the-art Cedrics team coach was approximately fourteen miles the other side of Kettering when the blaze drama unfolded. Initially, it was thought that the microwave in the kitchen area at the back of the coach had malfunctioned when several players reported a strong smell of burning around midnight. Minutes later, everyone realised that the problem was far more serious when the fumes began to spread through the coach. Luckily, Marc 'Malteser Head' Marangou and his co-driver Dave Humphreys were able to guide the coach into a side road only seconds before all the lights went out and the main batteries went up in flames. The two drivers put the fire out, but the coach was no longer serviceable. A replacement from a local company was hired to complete the journey, arriving back in Colchester at four o'clock in the morning.

Davison said: "We were in the middle of nowhere when the coach suddenly filled with smoke and acidic fumes. It was hammering down rain, but we all got off and stood outside while the fire was put out. It could have been very dangerous, but all's well that ends well and I eventually got home at the same time as the milkman was doing his round."

U's captain, Karl Duguid, said: "At first everyone could see the funny side of it and we all had a laugh, but then we all got the hump. What a way to finish the night!"

CHAPTER 23
SO WHAT REALLY
HAPPENED THEN?

It is often said in football – did he walk or was he pushed?

That was definitely the question in point following the departure of Colchester United managers Mike Walker and Steve Whitton.

Even today mystery still surrounds Walker's dismissal. The club issued a statement at the time that the Welshman's departure was a resignation, while a furious Walker phoned the *Gazette* the next day insisting he had been sacked.

Walker's team had seen-off Darlington 2-1 at Layer Road the day before and the next day – Sunday, 1 November 1987 – he was summoned to chairman Jonathan Crisp's home after taking a U's team to mark the official opening of Burnham Ramblers new ground in mid-Essex.

What happened at the meeting nobody knows to this day, but the exciting U's were top of the table and Walker was about to be named the October Fourth Division Manager of the Month. Rumours were rife regarding the reasons for Walker's departure, one being that chairman Crisp believed the only way out of Fourth Division football was to kick your way out.

Walker's team were playing some adventurous football in front of pathetic home crowds of no more than 1,200 thanks to Crisp's ill-judged decision to install a 100 per cent membership scheme if the fans wanted to watch matches at Layer Road. I had to interview the chairman soon after that and put it to him that his adventurous team must have been playing eye-catching football to be at the top.

"We're only top because of the number of penalties we've been awarded," he said – ironically only two when I counted.

I replied, "Well it showed we must have been playing attacking football to get so many players in the opponents' penalty box!"

Silence was the reply.

A similar set of circumstances surrounded Whitton's departure in January 2003. The club put out a circular that the pair had parted company by mutual consent, but when I phoned Steve for a comment, he told me exclusively, "I didn't walk away from it, I was sacked.

"When the phone went summoning me to a board meeting I knew what it meant. I've just experienced my first sacking and I'm out of a job for the first time in my life. I'd gone through the ranks at Colchester as a player, coach and manager and there's no way I was about to walk away from all that.

"When you become a manager though, you know there is nowhere else to go when things don't work out and right now I am consumed by three different moods – anger, relief and a little bit of limbo."

Threatened by relegation at the time, Whitton left the club after a managerial reign lasting three and a half seasons.

CHAPTER 24
WADSWORTH ALWAYS
BOUNCES BACK

Mick Wadsworth most definitely was not the most popular person during his short reign as manager of Colchester United!

The gritty, no-nonsense northerner managed to upset all and sundry during his short and stormy seven months in charge at Layer Road, but he has always maintained an uncanny knack of bouncing back – very often in much better jobs.

The former Carlisle and Scarborough boss was a surprise choice to step into Steve Wignall's shoes as the U's manager and his collection of nondescript signings failed to excite the fans who had been used to watching relative success during the previous manager's reign.

Wadsworth – a very nice well educated man away from football – brought in favourite old players of his, plus three untried French youngsters of whom only Thomas Pinault blossomed into a half-tidy midfielder. He also brought in unknown Irishman Brian Launders, who landed the club with a hefty legal bill following his instant sacking one Friday morning and the court cases that ensued.

Wadsworth's role came to an end on Tuesday night, 24 August 1999 when he was replaced by his assistant, Steve Whitton, following the U's 3-1 Worthington Cup defeat by Crystal Palace at Selhurst Park. Not to be outdone, he immediately set himself up with a coaching job at Palace before former Newcastle boss Bobby

Robson made him his assistant at St James' Park – Wadsworth having impressed Robson as a member of the national set-up during his tenure as England manager.

From Newcastle he moved to Southampton where he was assistant manager before moving on again to manage Oldham Athletic and Huddersfield. In November 2003, Wadsworth was named as the new National Football Coach of the Democratic Republic of the Congo where he teamed up once again with former Colchester United whiz-kid Lomana Tresor Lua Lua. Wadsworth promptly named Lua Lua as his captain.

That role lasted for just one season before our man popped up again as manager of Portuguese club Beira-Mar, quickly followed by another coaching role with Shrewsbury Town. After that he moved on again to take charge of now defunct Scottish League club, Gretna, in 2008.

Chester City followed in 2009 after which Wadsworth became team boss at Hartlepool for the 2010-11 campaign. The itchy feet were still there though and his next club was Cumbrian Northern League outfit Celtic Nation. They too folded last season!

Not to be outdone Wadsworth has bounced back yet again – this time as the current first team coach at Sheffield United. Phew – he's hard to keep up with!

CHAPTER 25
MANAGER MERRY-GO-ROUND

Colchester United have had thirty-two official managers since the club was formed back in 1937 and, if you take into account the caretaker bosses, that figure rises to forty-six.

In my time at the *Gazette* I worked with twelve of them, plus Steve Foley, who acted as caretaker manager no fewer than three times; Dale Roberts who filled the breach once, plus Steve Whitton and Micky Cook who filled the post for one match in January 1999.

We at the *Gazette* had to pull out all the stops whenever an old team boss moved on and a new one was appointed. The U's board of directors used to glory in our speculation as we fumbled around trying to get any clue as to who a new incumbent would be. They never told us a thing, or gave us a clue, as we chased up this lead and then another before ending up with the all-important name – or finishing up in the proverbial dead end.

When I questioned one director as to why the club never confirmed or denied any of the names we came up with he told me we love to see who you put in the frame and then chuckle to ourselves when you're way off the mark.

Only once in my time was the *Gazette* beaten, in fact the entire media circus had no idea who was going to replace Roy McDonough until George Burley emerged from behind a curtain. One-up to Layer Road chairman Gordon Parker! The rest of the time we were pretty much on the money – even if we did leave it until the eleventh hour a couple of times.

Here is the list of U's managers who kept me on my toes, brightened my working life, some becoming lifelong friends:

MIKE WALKER – a great guy to talk to with a wonderful outlook on the way to play football. He succeeded against all the odds in taking the U's to the top of the table before he was mysteriously and unceremoniously sacked. Mike went on to better things with Norwich City and even took the Canaries into Europe.

ROGER BROWN – the *Gazette* nailed down Roger 'Who' on the eve of his U's appointment thanks to a chance phone call to the Poole Town chairman. Poor old Roger tried hard, but he didn't have a clue and some of his tactics and signings were unbelievable. He took Walker's table-topping squad down into the depths of the Fourth Division only to stun us all at one February Press conference by boasting "PROMOTION! We're not only going to go up we're going to go up as CHAMPIONS!" Jolly Roger bit the dust ten games into the following season after a disastrous 8-0 defeat at Leyton Orient.

JOCK WALLACE – from Scottish giants Glasgow Rangers to Division Four minnows Colchester United. That was the path the legendary Wallace took in January 1989. If Brown was chalk, Jock was most definitely cheese and the gritty ex-goalkeeper proved exactly that. His tough clenched fist image and strong inspirational talk galvanised all around him, but as his health began to fail so Jock was forced to call it a day eleven months later.

MICK MILLS – the ex-England and Ipswich Town captain was chairman Jonathan Crisp's next surprise choice, but the struggling U's were already heading for the GM Vauxhall Conference and Mills' quietly-spoken uninspiring style failed to lift the players and fans alike. Crisp said the U's couldn't afford a manager of Mills' qualities.

IAN ATKINS – canny 'Brummy' Atkins – currently employed as the full time European Senior Scout for Everton – was lured away from Ipswich to become player-manager for the U's first season of Conference football and he laid the foundations for what was to follow twelve months later. A talented player and great communicator, sadly, for Atkins his quest for glory fell agonisingly short, but he had made his mark and quit to join his home town club Birmingham City at the end of the season.

ROY McDONOUGH – not everybody's cup of tea as a manager, but brought in by Atkins as a player the previous season 'Big Roy's all-action attacking style promptly paid dividends as he spearheaded the U's to a glorious Wembley final triumph and the GM Vauxhall Conference and FA Trophy double.

Great for the fans and great for the local newspaper and, according to skipper Tony English, he was great for the players. Expecting to get a bollicking after a hefty defeat at Welling, English said Roy turned up for training the next day and took the heat right out of the moment by saying, "Right lads, let's go and play a game of cricket." That's man management for you!

Roy was always available but, sadly for him, he was

given the order of the boot after guiding the club into a respectable mid-table position after their first season back in the Football League.

GEORGE BURLEY – the surprise of all surprises, plucked out of the obscurity of Scottish League football as boss of Ayr United, the U's gave him his first chance of Football League management. He had a great knack for talking a lot and telling you nothing, but after a poor start he guided the club into the Fourth Division promotion play-off places before walking out on the U's in mid-season to manage Ipswich Town, the team he had represented so magnificently as a player.

STEVE WIGNALL – in my view, the U's most successful manager ever with two Wembley finals – the Auto Windscreens Shield final and Division Three Promotion Play-Off final – one promotion, two promotion play-off semi-finals, plus one near miss by a solitary point of a third play-off semi-final.

A huge favourite with the fans during his seven years at Layer Road as a player, Wiggy earned his managerial spurs by guiding non-league Aldershot to two unexpected promotions. Disillusioned by a failure to bring in new players that he wanted because of financial restraints at the U's he eventually resigned after five years at the helm.

MICK WADSWORTH – never a great favourite with the fans, the much-travelled northerner upset too many people during his short seven-month stay at the club. He got rid of existing popular players and replaced them with dodgy foreigners – untried French players – plus two or three of his old favourites.

I, personally, enjoyed a good relationship with Mick

despite his questionable ideas on how the team should be run. He disappeared under a cloud five games into the 1999-2000 season.

STEVE WHITTON – signed by McDonough as a U's player in the club's first season back in the Football League, the former West Ham, Coventry City, Birmingham, Sheffield Wednesday and Ipswich Town star worked wonders on a shoestring budget.

Former Liverpool and Denmark star Jan Molby, ex-Barnsley boss Steve Parkin, Dagenham and Redbridge chief Garry Hill and Southend United coach Stewart Robson were all in the frame to fill Whitton's shoes.

PHIL PARKINSON – the U's sprung yet another surprise when naming the thirty-five-year-old untried Reading player-coach as their new boss. Handpicked by U's chairman Peter Heard one was given the impression that he didn't want his man to fail and Parky appeared to get resources other Layer Road managers had not.

A good man to talk to, Parky often took a lot to heart and he told me to stop phoning him one day and go away and do my job properly. When I phoned him the next day to say is it right you are looking to sign former Chelsea defender Andy Myers from Bradford City he said, "Where did you get that from? I don't want that printed because I don't want other clubs to know he's available."

"I did my job properly, Phil, like you suggested," I said to him.

To which he replied, "I promise you the exclusive when I do sign Myers if you sit on the story."

He kept his word. Sadly, he too left under a cloud after guiding the U's into the Championship in only his third full season in charge.

GERAINT WILLIAMS – served the club as a player and then player-coach to both Whitton and Parkinson and the former Ipswich Town, Derby County, Bristol Rovers and Wales international midfielder fully deserved his first chance at management as Parky's successor.

One of the nicest men you could ever wish to meet, he guided the U's into tenth spot in his first full season as a Championship manager, but poor gates and a lack of more players took their toll and he too departed.

STEVE FOLEY – never officially appointed as manager, former striker and youth team coach Foley enjoyed three spells as caretaker spanning the departure of Mike Walker to the appointment of Roy McDonough.

A very popular figure around Layer Road, Foley always got the crowd going with his attractive brand of adventurous football and, in the loan signing of West Bromwich Albion midfielder Tony Kelly, he brought to Layer Road one of the finest footballers ever seen in U's colours.

DALE ROBERTS – a close ally of George Burley, the talented and likeable Roberts held the reins as caretaker for just two matches before quitting after the U's FA Cup defeat against Wimbledon at Selhurst Park.

Since I quit my U's football role at the *Gazette*, Colchester have appointed seven more managers – Paul Lambert, Aidy Boothroyd, John Ward, Joe Dunne, Tony Humes, Kevin Keen and John McGreal.

I also had the pleasure of speaking to many other old favourites such as Bobby Roberts, the breath of fresh air that was Jim Smith and, of course, the one and only, dear old Dick Graham.

Bobby Roberts did extremely well on a very low

budget, while former Boston United boss Smith livened up the squad with extremely talented players such as striker John Froggatt and little football wizard Bobby Svarc. Both Roberts and Smith won the U's promotion.

Dick Graham was a legend and still is. He only ever won the Watney Cup, but he built a great team of older players, including England international centre-forward Ray Crawford, that took the U's into the FA Cup quarter-finals as a Fourth Division side, beating reigning star-studded English champions Leeds United along the way. I spent many an hour chatting to Dick and both he and I loved it.

Characters like Dick are few and far between these days and the game of football is all the poorer for it.

CHAPTER 26
U'S DAVID LOOKS AFTER
THE BIG BOYS NOW

I wonder how many Colchester United fans remember the club's Chief Executive David Barnard?

I also wonder how many of them are now aware that 'Our David' has since moved on from bottom of the old Fourth Division football to the lofty heights of European Champions League football as club secretary at former Premier League champions Chelsea.

Nobody can ever accuse David of not having experienced the ups and downs of our wonderful game. Barnard arrived at Colchester as Chief Executive from Fulham in the summer of 1987, after learning of the vacancy from U's reserve team coach Colin Henson during the annual Zeebrugge Youth Tournament in Holland. One of his first roles was to clear up the mess left by Mike Walker's mystery sacking in October and the arrival of new team boss Roger Brown.

Barnard remained with the U's until they were relegated out of the Football League at the end of the 1989-90 season. He moved on to Wimbledon as their Chief Exec until moving on to become Club Secretary of Chelsea in 2002.

So, after experiencing the lows of relegation out of the League he has enjoyed the thrills of seeing his current club win almost everything there is to win. He has seen Chelsea crowned Premier League champions four times, FA Cup winners six times, League Cup winners four times, FA Charity Shield winners three times, Full

Members Cup winners once, UEFA Champions League champions once, UEFA Europa League champions once, UEFA Cup Winners Cup Winners once and UEFA Super Cup once.

On the darker side, he found himself in deep trouble from the Football Association following his handling of the John Terry, Ashley Cole/Anton Ferdinand racial abuse affair.

Fortunately, he came out of the argument unscathed in the end.

CHAPTER 27
WATCH YOUR BACK PONDER

Have you ever faced the threat of a knife being plunged between your shoulder blades?

I have! It happened back in November 1995 after the U's and Exeter City fans ran riot inside the Layer Road ground. The two sets of fans had been taunting each other straight from the kick-off and at half-time a fight broke out when a small group of 'Barside' thugs launched a pitch invasion and stole a flag from an Exeter supporter. The flag had been prominently displayed in the home supporters' area and was set alight causing a fire risk and antagonising the away fans.

Police and club stewards moved in to weed out the hooligans, prompting U's chairman Gordon Parker to lament: "Regrettably the more media coverage these louts get the more they like it. The repercussions of these unfortunate incidents are the £20,000 to £30,000 their disgusting behaviour may cost the club in future extra police costs."

Parker's words were roundly echoed by U's boss Steve Wignall, who said: "I thought all those dark days had gone. All those idiot fans have succeeded in doing is to jeopardise my chances of receiving money for new players."

Skipper Tony English threw his weight firmly behind the manager saying, "Once again the loutish minority will grab all the headlines while the team and the genuine fans suffer."

However, it was the comment piece I was ordered to write by my editor that led to my stabbing threat. It read like this:

'Kick these scum supporters out of Layer Road now before they blacken the name of Colchester United beyond reproach and cost the club a fortune it can ill afford in football fines and police costs. The mindless morons' manic behaviour was disgraceful and sickening to watch – and for what? An Exeter City supporter's pathetic flag!

Yes, our big brave babies – for that's all they are – cast the club into disrepute with the police and the Football Association all for the sake of a flag. I hope you're proud of your loutish kindergarten prank boys – or should I re-spell that and brand you for what you are – YOBS! Only the dummies and dirty nappies were missing – although I wouldn't be too sure of that!

You can't even blame police harassment this time, yobs, because the cops weren't even in the ground at the time. So what's your excuse – did the Exeter mob dent your pathetic childish pride, or were you just spoiling for a fight?

Whatever the reason there's no place at Layer Road for cowardly thugs, vermin, hooligans, morons, louts, yobs – call'em what you like – even plain and simple prats, at a time when the club is striving to attract more fans to watch its matches. The club doesn't want you and the thousands of decent fans don't want their reputation tarnished by a handful of idiots like you.

If it's a fight you bullies want why don't you try one of the American style boot camps, or even the local army glasshouse. The authorities there will quickly show you how brave you really are.

So grow up and get lost before the police sure as hell catch up with you – as they most definitely will.'

The phone rang on Monday morning to reveal a cowardly thuggish voice threatening me with the promise, "Step outside your office, Ponder, and you'll get a knife between your shoulder blades!"

I vividly remember my response. I said, "If I was scared of cowardly louts like you I wouldn't have written my comment piece in the first place!"

The phone went quiet.

CHAPTER 28
SURFING THE BBC ESSEX AIRWAVES

He's always heard, but never seen – and he's worked at some of the best and worst professional football grounds in the country. His name is my good mate Neil Kelly, the radio voice of Colchester United, and his chocolate-rich, north-eastern tones can be heard by the thousands of BBC Essex listeners as he relays live commentary on the U's matches throughout the football season.

He has, what I call, a great radio voice, but his regular day job is a teacher of history and politics and Head of Student Services at Colchester's Sixth Form College, where a friend, BBC journalist Christine Garrington, urged him to try his hand at radio.

Neil, born 250 miles away in Hartlepool, yet having spent more than half his life in Essex, will be the first to tell you he's not had any radio coaching or tuition. The same could be said of me when I enjoyed my first broadcast as a summarizer for Neil at the ripe old age of forty-six.

When I was a kid I never in my entire life expected to hear myself blabbing on the radio, but suddenly it became a regular occurrence – mostly at the U's away matches when, as the *Evening Gazette*'s Colchester United correspondent and match reporter, I was so often called upon.

It was hard because the concentration levels were so high, but I loved it and when the good feedback from family, friends, workmates and fans throughout the county came flooding in I couldn't get enough of it. To this day though I'm glad I was a written word sports journalist, but the radio experience was simply fantastic.

Neil and I had a great rapport behind the microphone. We tried to make our broadcasts entertaining, informative and funny. On that score, he was a bit of a bugger and, knowing full well that I had my head down sometimes, collating the notes for my *Gazette* report, he would nudge me and say, "What happened there, Francis?"

He was also a great supporter of me and quite often listeners would phone into the studio and tell the anchorman to get Ponder off the radio. "The man's a jinx," they so often said. "Every time he opens his mouth something bad happens."

I can remember one particular match when a caller phoned in and said, "Ponder's a disaster, get him off."

To which Neil replied on air, "That's strange because I've been sitting beside him all afternoon and he hasn't put a foot wrong, made a poor pass, or a bad tackle."

On another occasion I was working with BBC Essex commentator Steve Houghton up among the gods at Swansea's run-down Vetch Field stadium for a first round FA Cup-tie in November 1999. The U's were more than holding their own when Lomana Tresor Lua Lua scored a great goal to put them in front with just over thirty minutes to play.

As the tie entered the final ten minutes, Steve turned to me and said, "It's looking good, Francis, what do you think?"

I'd hardly got the words, "It's looking like a great win here," out of my mouth when Swansea netted their equaliser.

"Get him off!" came the call from the listeners again.

Steve said, "Don't take any notice of them," and, as we entered the final few minutes he turned and said to me, It's looking good now."

I replied, "At least we'll take them back to Layer Road for a replay."

The word replay had barely left my lips when Swansea netted a last minute winner and the phones became red hot again – as if it was all my fault!

Looking back, it was so easy to upset a lot of fans on away grounds because our commentary position was only too often situated right in the middle of them in the main stand. Neil's voice is quite strong and my heart was in my mouth more than once as I could see what he was saying was getting up the nose of a lot of them.

I distinctly recall a game at Cardiff or Wrexham when a home club season ticket holder kept turning round looking at where we were sitting. He suddenly got up, approached Neil and said, "If you don't shut your mouth I'll shut it for you. I'm fed-up of listening to your voice."

Quick as a flash Neil responded, "Don't blame me, mate, blame your club. They stuck me here!" We never heard from that guy again.

I have worked with many a good sports guy at BBC Essex, including Nick Atkins, Andy Kay, Glenn Speller, Ben Fryer, Stuart Smith, Robin Chipperfield, Roger Buxton, Steve Houghton, Shaun Peel (now a *BBC Look East* TV presenter), Jonathan Overend (now BBC 5 Live) and Mark Pougatch (currently plying his trade between Radio 5 Live and as ITV's anchorman for their football coverage).

I'm so glad BBC Essex gave me the opportunity to have a go at it. There was no better feeling to see the U's playing so well, which really got the adrenaline flowing, as we broadcast the action to the fans back home in Colchester and the surrounding areas.

CHAPTER 29
COMEDY OF ERRORS

The last four seasons of Colchester United football have been hell to watch if you are a U's fan.

The League One club managed to avoid relegation by the skin of its teeth for three of the last four seasons. The 2014-15 season was the closest yet with relegation only staved off on the final day with a great 1-0 home win over promotion chasing Preston North End.

Even that had a big slice of luck about it because if Notts County and Crawley Town had won their last games they would have stayed in League One. Luckily for the U's, they both lost and went down, but if they had won it wouldn't have mattered how many goals Colchester had beaten Preston by – it would have been the U's who went down instead.

Sadly, the lessons still hadn't been learned and, for the fourth time in as many years, the Essex side was once again fighting an uphill battle to avoid the drop into League Two football.

Lady luck, however, ran out on them and the U's relegation was eventually confirmed well before the end of the season.

As a fan, I have witnessed some woeful displays over the past four seasons, but I can't help thinking the local press and radio – including my old paper the *Colchester Gazette* – have let the team off very lightly. I could never remember being so tame with my reaction, so off up into my loft I went to seek out some of the headlines that accompanied my match reports – and I'm happy to say that I and my sub-editors didn't pull any punches.

How's this for starters, 'Comedy of errors no fun for poor fans' (at best woeful at worst comical) following a 2-1 home defeat at the hands of Scarborough.

'It's a festive fiasco' (what a let-down for biggest crowd) following a drab goalless home draw with Mansfield Town.

'Roy should drop the lot of them!' After U's fans suffered a 4-2 home defeat against Wrexham.

'Worst yet from abysmal U's after a 3-1 setback at Scunthorpe.'

'Uninspiring shambles' following another 0-0 home draw with Bury.

'BLUE MURDER' (Basement club beat sorry U's 7-3) after humiliating display at Darlington. (U's let in seven...and the goalie is their star man) from the same match.

'No method, no passion, no good!' Following the U's FA Cup demise at home to Gillingham.

'It's the same old story' as York City win 2-0.

'I WOULDN'T HAVE PAID TO WATCH' (Rubbish football; upsets U's boss) after 1-1 home draw with Barnet.

'Hopeless U's humbled' after Gravesend and Northfleet knocked them out of the FA Cup.

'ZERO POINTS FOR EFFORT' after 3-1 home defeat to Stoke City.

'Diabolical and gutless U's given a lesson in passion' (woeful-diabolical-gutless-pathetic) after 3-1 defeat at Peterborough.

'Boos and jeers for listless U's' after 3-1 home defeat by Lincoln City.

'Gutless, inept and embarrassing (the U's fielded far too many players who lacked stomach or passion to fight it out)' after 2-0 defeat at Macclesfield.

'Woeful U's just haven't a clue' following a 3-0 home

defeat to Bristol Rovers.

'Hung, drawn and slaughtered' after 5-1 home thrashing by Gillingham.

There were many, many, more and I dread to think what my tally of scathing headlines would have been had I still been reporting on the U's for the last four seasons.

CHAPTER 30
POCKET DYNAMO

Colchester United came within an ace of signing £21 million rated, former England, Manchester City and Chelsea wonder-winger Shaun Wright-Phillips!

The shock deal was almost pulled off back in July 2005 when Wright-Phillips was a budding thirteen-year-old youth player, disillusioned with his lot at then Premier League club Nottingham Forest.

Pocket-dynamo Wright-Phillips – the adopted son of former England and Arsenal star Ian Wright – opted instead to sign for Manchester City, who had been pursuing him for some time.

U's Youth Development officer at the time, Geoff Harrop, said, "The standing joke then was that Manchester City offered Shaun the world and we at Colchester couldn't match that – or more to the point, City offered him and his family a luxury holiday in Barbados. We could only offer them a week in Clacton!"

Harrop, the man who originally spotted former U's and Newcastle ace Lomana Tresor Lua Lua, told the *Gazette*, "We came very close to signing Shaun. I had connections with his boys club in London, Ten-Em-Bee. His brother Bradley was also there at the time and we offered Shaun an opportunity to come and have a look at how we did things at Colchester. He was very special then. Technically he was excellent. Small, compact and very quick with two great feet, a brilliant touch and tons of pace.

"Nottingham Forest didn't want to let him go, but Shaun enjoyed a lovely time with us. He was like a little powder keg ready to explode and, like Lua Lua, he always played with a great big smile on his face."

Former U's youth supremo Micky Cook said, "You could never say Shaun was the future big fish that got away. He was fully locked in at Nottingham Forest at the time and came to us on the pathway through his footballing life. He was so tiny, a little pocket-sized atom bomb just waiting to go off at any time. When you've got speed and power like him it doesn't matter how big or small you are.

"Shaun has always been outside the stereotype."

Wright-Phillips – capped six times at Under-21 level and 36 times as a full England international – made 153 appearances for Manchester City before moving to Chelsea for £21 million in July 2005 where he made a further eighty-one appearances.

He returned to Manchester City in August 2008 for an undisclosed transfer fee, believed to be in the region of £8.5 million, where he made another sixty-five appearances, before transferring to Queens Park Rangers for an undisclosed fee in August 2011 where he made sixty-seven League and cup outings.

He was among a host of QPR players released from their contracts before he signed for American Major Soccer League outfit New York Red Bulls where he made only twelve appearances before being released at the end of the 2015 season.

CHAPTER 31
WEMBLEY WOE

Sunday, 10 May 1992. The town was awash with blue and white – the triumphant colours of newly crowned GM Vauxhall Conference champions, Colchester United.

Everyone was in a buoyant mood as the jubilant U's prepared for the greatest day in their fifty-five-year history – they were off to the world famous Wembley Stadium where only Witton Albion stood in their way of completing a glorious Conference and FA Trophy double. Roy McDonough's men duly completed the task ahead of them, but for one man – U's defensive midfielder Shaun Elliott – the day was one he couldn't wait to forget.

England B international Elliott had played all but a handful of games for the U's that season and he confessed to being totally shattered when Layer Road player-manager McDonough told him he was not in his starting line-up for the Trophy final.

"I was furious, totally gutted, very screwed up about it," said Shaun. "The day still rankles greatly with me and even today I'm still very angry that I didn't get to play at Wembley. Roy (McDonough) had brought in Dave Martin from Southend seemingly under the proviso that, if we got to Wembley, he would play him.

"The manager did say I could be one of his substitutes if I wanted to, but having already missed the 1985 Milk Cup final between two of my old clubs, Sunderland and Norwich, because of suspension I didn't want to go to Wembley to sit on the bench again.

"I was captain of Sunderland at the time," said the

119

former England Under-21 international, "and I had never felt so disappointed and empty. Wembley is no place to go unless you are playing, so I missed the trip with Colchester completely and I never played for the club again."

Shaun made 419 Football League appearances, 321 for Sunderland, thirty-one for Norwich and sixty-seven for Blackpool, earning seven England Under-21 international caps and three England B caps, against Spain (twice) and the USA along the way.

He joined the U's on a free transfer from Blackpool (Colchester having to fork out £7,000 to the Seasiders for his services four months later) after Ian Atkins, U's player-boss at the time, made it known he was looking for a centre-half.

"I was good friends with Ackers when I played with him at Sunderland," said Shaun, "and he persuaded me to sign for Colchester."

Elliott played a total of sixty-one Conference and cup games for the U's before his departure, having failed to agree terms for the U's first season back in the Football League.

"Football has certainly changed a lot since then," he said, "and I would have loved the chance to be earning more than £20,000 a week playing football. "Good players, even in my day, made a lot of money out of the game."

CHAPTER 32
SUPER SHILTS

It's not common practice for a top international footballer to hand out his home telephone number to a newspaper reporter he has never met!

Perhaps I was born lucky, or he simply liked the sound of my voice, but that's exactly what England's most capped goalkeeper – 125 – Peter Shilton OBE did.

Shilts was only four games away from creating a fantastic historic record of 1,000 Football League and Premiership appearances when he replied to the fax I had sent to West Ham's training ground seeking an interview with him.

"I can't talk to you now," said Peter on the phone, "but here's my home number. Ring me back at three o'clock when I've finished training and we'll have plenty of time to talk then."

The Hammers were suffering a goalkeeper injury crisis at the start of the 1996-97 season and Shilts – who was due to play in the U's former West Ham striker Steve Whitton's August Testimonial at Layer Road – had answered an SOS from Upton Park boss Harry Redknapp at the time.

As he approached his unique milestone around the time of his forty-seventh birthday, plus his thirtieth season in League football, the former Leicester, Stoke, Nottingham Forest, Southampton, Derby, Plymouth and Bolton keeper told me, "The match at Colchester was my first eleven-a-side game of any description for months. Everything fell into place so naturally, however, I felt as though I had been playing forever.

"Of course it would have been nice to have played those four games with West Ham to become the first player to reach 1,000 and, although records have never worried me throughout my career, 1,000 games is somewhat special and it's a milestone I'm determined to achieve.

"While I feel as good as I do I will carry on playing, preferably in the Premier League. I want to carry on playing at the top level as long as I can. West Ham have offered me a deal for the first five months of the 1996-97 season, but the way I feel right now I still have a good three years goalkeeping left in me at the top level which will take me up to my fiftieth birthday."

A two-time European Cup winner, UEFA Super Cup winner, English Championship and League Cup winner with Nottingham Forest, Shilton said he would willingly drop down into the Football League to achieve his dream of completing a record 1,000 matches.

"I was very impressed with the goal Colchester scored against me in Steve Whitton's Testimonial," he said. "The fact they are clearly a club that likes to play football, I wouldn't hesitate to help out a nice little team like them in an emergency. They are not one of those teams that hacks the ball down the channels for somebody to chase and, the lad that knocked in their goal against me put the ball in the only spot that was going to beat me."

As things turned out, West Ham's Czech international keeper Ludo Miklosko was fit enough to take his place between the sticks at the start of the season so Peter Shilton had to wait a little while longer to clock up his record 1,000.

His big moment came on 22 December 1996 in a 2-0 home win for Leyton Orient against Division Three rivals Brighton and Hove Albion. He went on to make five more League appearances for the O's.

Peter said "My general fitness and sharpness don't appear to be any different from when I first broke into professional football. The great Sir Stanley Matthews played League football until he was fifty and I still feel as I did ten years ago – very fit and raring to go."

Shilton's record 1,000 was completed as follows – Leicester City (286), Stoke City (110), Nottingham Forest (202), Southampton (188), Derby County (175), Plymouth Argyle (34), Bolton Wanderers (1), Leyton Orient (9) = 1,005.

CHAPTER 33
CHIRPY AND THE CHEEP-CHEEPS

Wembley three times; relegation out of the Football League; promotion back into the League; promotion twice more and promotion play-offs twice!

Not a bad record for a female in a man's world who has seen off fifteen managers – plus three caretaker-managers – and has also waved cheerio to five chairmen.

There can't be too many Football League chief executives who can boast a record as colourful as that and that comes from a chief executive who at one time didn't know much about football!

MARIE PARTNER – the First Lady of Colchester United Football Club.

Marie rose through the ranks from commercial office assistant to commercial manager, club secretary, managing director and then chief executive – taking in such extra roles as agony aunt and surrogate mum to the players. There were other women before her such as Betty Scott, Dee Ellwood and Sue Smith, who reached the lofty heights of U's secretary, but fitness fanatic Marie topped the lot.

Marie was a mere slip of a girl when she first walked into Layer Road as part of an all-female teeny-bopper dance group who called themselves Chirpy (Marie) and the Cheep-Cheeps – the fill-in act between *Flash Gordon* and the adverts at Colchester Odeon's Saturday Morning Kids' Club. Little did she know it then, but she was later going to spend a big part of her life in the homely old stadium.

Marie, who started work at Layer Road on the same day as the legendary manager Jock Wallace, quit her job after twenty-one years at the club and she is just one of so many U's stars and characters who came into my working life.

BRIAN OWEN – known by us all as simply BO.

Been there and done it all, Brian holds the unique record of having been a player, physio and coach in all four divisions of English league football – you can probably add scout to that list as well!

BO also dabbled in the England international set-up and what he doesn't know about football isn't worth knowing. He also boasts a strong knowledge of the national political scene as well.

A real man's man, BO was always great to be around.

DAVID BLACKNALL – top class groundsman and stadium manager.

Modest and hard-working, there's nothing David can't put his hand to as you would expect from a man trained at Nottingham Forest in the Brian Clough era.

JOHN BROOKE – kit manager and general go-to man. A lovely bloke with a great sense of humour, the late John and I spent a lot of time chatting about all and sundry on the team coach and I was only too ready to help him lay out the players' kit and boots on the U's away days.

Like David Blacknall, John was a great handyman who became my great friend.

MARC MARANGOU – U's team coach driver, always known to me as 'Malteser Head' because his head was as round and as brown as the popular chocolate sweet.

I spent hours sitting in the courier's seat alongside Marc talking about everything from music, his job, to the state of the world in general. We even spent hours playing motorway cricket as we went along – one run for every black car; two for a grey or silver, three for a red; four for a blue and so on. An Eddie Stobart lorry meant you were out.

Old 'Malteser Head' was full of tricks though, as he proved one night on the way home from an away game. I had just emerged from the toilet near the back of the bus when he spotted me in his mirror, jammed his brakes on sharply and then spurted forward again, sending me flying, arse first, into a box of fruit under the kitchen sink right at the rear of the coach. I can still hear his inane laughter now!

PETER WRIGHT – the late, great speedy left-winger.

Peter was voted by the *Gazette* readers as the U's Player of the 20th Century. Always in our office, he was a great friend to me and together we sowed the first seeds for, what has become known as, the Colchester United Former Players Association, an association he was very proud of.

The statue erected in his honour where the old Layer Road pitch used to be is a fitting tribute to such a great man.

VIC KEEBLE – super star, ordinary bloke.

Vic thought nothing of travelling to matches at Layer Road on the same Colchester Corporation bus as the U's fans in his playing days.

Now eighty-five-years-old, he put the club on the map back in 1952 with his £15,000 transfer to north-eastern giants Newcastle United with whom he won an FA Cup winners' medal in 1955. Vic had the honour of netting the U's first hat-trick in the Football League (against Plymouth Argyle in 1951).

He is another 'Golden Oldie' I got to know well.

BOBBY HUNT – still holds the U's record for the most goals scored in a season.

A keen all-round sportsman in his heyday, Bobby is a really good friend and can still be seen in the main stand at every home match.

REG STEWART – lived and breathed Colchester United until his untimely death.

Your typical gruff northerner, lofty club captain Reg was a big hit with the fans back in the 1950s for his no-nonsense displays at the heart of the U's defence.

Yet another great friend of mine.

PAUL DYER – motor-mouth Paul never stops talking and, it has been said, he bored his opponents to death in his playing days.

Also known as Spam, he served the club both as a defensive midfielder and later chief scout. Life is never quiet when Paul is about!

RAY CRAWFORD – a Cup hero of the famous 1971 Leeds tie, larger than life Ray says he still eats out on his exploits in that game. Living in the Portsmouth area, he's always available whenever I phone him.

DAVE SIMMONS – the other scorer in that famous cup-tie.

Dave became not only a good friend, he also came to

live close by and we enjoyed endless chats about his life in pro football. Sadly, Dave died of cancer far too early.

ALBERT 'DIGGER' KETTLE – I got to know Digger very well when I wrote several features about Southern League U's famous FA Cup run back in 1947-48. Always popular with the fans for his all-action, non-stop displays, Digger became a legend around Layer Road.

BOB CURRY – captain and goal-getter back in that great FA Cup run. He was a great ambassador for the club in more ways than one.

Bob gave me the football – autographed by all the players – from the FA Cup quarter-final his U's team played at Blackpool. I later presented the ball to the club to place in their museum.

LEN 'SPUD' CATER – dashing left-winger.

Len loved to talk about the team's great FA Cup exploits of the late 1940s and he had a packed scrapbook for me to glean info from.

PAUL ROBERTS – the joker in the pack.

It was always a laugh a minute with Robbo, who was Roy McDonough's real Jack-the-Lad.

TREVOR PUTNEY – like Paul Roberts it was laugh a minute in Putters' company. He was a very talented footballer as well.

MARK KINSELLA – I was there when he signed as a mere teenage lad and there when he was transferred to Charlton Athletic. Mark was one of the finest players to don a U's shirt.

STEVE McGAVIN – another good friend who stepped out of non-league football to carve out a great professional career for himself.

PETER CAWLEY – larger than life Pete always played with his heart on his sleeve and a smile on his face which masked the hardman defender he really was.

My list of great characters and friends is endless. There are so many more I could name as well.

CHAPTER 34
ROBBO, CHRIS AND
JAMIE LETS RIP

The *Gazette* back page splash said it all on Friday, 13 May 1994 – ANGRY ROBERTS ATTACKS BOARD!

The U's are 'going backwards' says axed defender Paul Roberts.

Roberts' outburst followed the leaked news of his release – along with Alan Dickens – and the wage war which was erupting within the club as many of the remaining players disputed the terms of their new contracts.

"I really don't know what the club is trying to do," said Roberts, who was facing up to life on the scrapheap at the age of thirty-two.

And in a bitter broadside he warned the Layer Road board of directors: "Stop treading a path towards disaster and stop treating your players like second class citizens.

"If the board are trying to get rid of the club's experienced players to bring in cheap and untried youngsters they are going the right way about it."

That scenario rings a few bells right now in 2016!

Roberts added, "Far from being a formula for success I see it as a formula for doom – only this time I don't think the fans will get behind the club if it drops out of the League a second time. The board keep telling everyone they are ambitious, but what kind of incentive do the lads have to play well when they are being asked to accept a pay cut? Take me, for instance, I had to take a drop of £2,500 after finishing as the club's Player of the Season. What kind of incentive was that?

"Some lower non-league clubs offer better incentives than Colchester. The board has never been ready to speculate and a typical example of their ambition was to opt for the cheapest option in bringing in a Chelmsford City reserve team goalkeeper when we were lying fourth in the table.

"As far as I am concerned I feel very bitter at the way I have been shot out of the door, especially as one of the highest sources in the club always led me to believe there might be a coaching job for me at Layer Road if I earned my coaching badges. I am totally gutted because I feel the board led me up the garden path and now I fear others may follow."

Ironically for Roberts, although there might have been a lot of truth in what he claimed, the U's gradually went from strength to strength towards the Football League Championship – just one tier under the Premier League itself.

There were more harsh words and claims of 'lack of ambition from the U's board' thirteen years later as red-hot marksman Jamie Cureton and Chris Iwelumo ran into a brick wall when attempting to tie-up new contracts. The U's had not many weeks earlier finished a Football League season in their highest position ever – tenth in the Coca-Cola Championship!

Iwelumo – who was out of contract and being headhunted by the likes of Charlton Athletic, Leicester City, Wolverhampton Wanderers and Coventry City – warned the U's board the club should be looking after its players if they wished to remain a force in the game.

The giant goal-getter – brought back from German football to play for Colchester two years earlier by U's, then boss, Phil Parkinson – had already left the Essex club after failing to agree terms of a new deal.

Worried that his departure might signal a mass exodus by other U's players he warned, "The board of directors must start matching the players' and coaching staff's ambitions if they want to continue to move forward.

"After our achievements of the past two seasons the board should be doing a lot more to keep the squad together. I was amazed they didn't do more to keep me! Most clubs would die for a goal-scoring duo like myself and Jamie Cureton (forty-two goals for the season).

"We were envied by a lot of clubs in the Coca-Cola Championship and they would build around a partnership like that. I dread to think what will happen if another club comes in with a big money bid for Cureton? He has just won the 'Golden Boot' as the Championship's top scorer and the U's should be looking to reward him accordingly."

Disillusioned by the offer made to him, Iwelumo – nineteen goals in his first season and eighteen in the season just gone, including four in one game against Hull City – moved on to sign a new three-year contact with the U's Championship rivals Charlton, recently relegated out of the Premier League.

Iwelumo said: "People are accusing me of moving on just for the money – it couldn't be further from the truth. Obviously, the money has something to do with it, but I had struck-up a great understanding with Jamie Cureton and I didn't want to leave the way I did."

It took Cureton another week to break his silence, but clearly disheartened at losing his prolific strike partner he stunned the U's board with a transfer request.

He said: "I still had another twelve months to go on my current three-year deal, but I will be thirty-three-years-old when this runs out so I would like the opportunity now to talk to the bigger clubs who are interested in signing me."

The much-travelled striker's request for a move was promptly turned down, but it is believed bids from other clubs had already been received and Cureton hinted, "You are only worth what someone will pay for you. Colchester did offer me a new deal along with new terms for Kemi Izzet and Wayne Brown, even though I was still under contract, but I didn't think it was for me.

"I reached a situation earlier this summer where I sat down and took a good look at was left of my career for the future. I'm not selfish and I'm not silly. I know Colchester's situation and I know they can't match what the bigger teams are offering players. But I'm not twenty-one anymore and I know there's interest in me out there – this could be my last chance to play for a big club.

"I will always be very grateful that Colchester gave me a chance to play Championship football again, but I don't think they ever thought they might be selling me."

Cureton was snapped up soon after by one of his previous clubs, Norwich City, for a staggering transfer fee of £850,000.

CHAPTER 35
WARNOCK WAGES WAR

Colchester United chairman Gordon Parker branded Neil Warnock's behaviour an 'utter disgrace' minutes after the U's promotion dream died at Plymouth's Home Park back in May 1996.

The much travelled Warnock, manager of Argyle at the time, had incensed Parker following a confrontation with referee John Kirkby who he claimed had failed to send-off the U's central defender Tony McCarthy for a professional foul during the second half.

Warnock was ordered from the dugout following his comments, but Kirkby failed to send him right away deep into the back of the stands, allowing the home team boss to bark out orders to his team while standing just a couple of feet to the side.

One such order was not to give the ball back to Colchester from a throw-in after a U's player had put it into touch following an injury to a home player. His actions were accompanied by boos and jeers from all quarters of the ground, but Plymouth, who went into the second leg of this Division Three promotion play-off, 1-0 behind went on to snatch a place at Wembley with a 3-2 aggregate win.

Warrnock angered Parker further when saying, "When your side reaches the play-offs and you only bring a couple of hundred fans with you, well you don't deserve to be in a play-off final at Wembley."

Those comments provoked an immediate response from Parker who said: "Neil Warnock's behaviour as a manager was disgraceful. He might be going to

Wembley, but I know which manager I would prefer to have."

Stunned U's boss Steve Wignall refused to comment on Warnock's antics.

The loud-mouthed Plymouth boss had already upset the Colchester camp by accusing the Layer Road fans of throwing apple cores at his players during the first leg of the tie, which the U's won 1-0 courtesy of a stunning lone Mark Kinsella goal. The clearly rattled Pilgrims chief then added insult to injury by suggesting the U's were favourites to win the second leg.

WHO ARE YOU KIDDING? Splashed the *Gazette*'s back page headline!

Not bad for a manager whose club had already informed the FA they wanted 35,000 tickets for the Wembley final!

Warnock had also told the media after the first leg: "Little clubs such as Colchester have no right to be sharing the same pitch as his Plymouth all-stars."

Although Kinsella gave the U's some hope of reaching the final after scoring again late in the second leg the West Country club marched on to Wembley thanks to goals from Michael Evans, Chris Leadbitter and Paul Williams, the last one coming just five minutes before the end.

Both Warnock and Wignall had already tasted play-off final success. Warnock guided both Huddersfield and Notts County to Wembley triumphs, while Wignall was a key member of the Aldershot side that had beaten both Bolton Wanderers and the much fancied Wolves to win the Division Four play-off final.

Warnock's Plymouth met Darlington, semi-final victors over Hereford, in the final.

CHAPTER 36
MY BEST U'S TEAM
SPANNING 1985-2005
(MY YEARS AS THE GAZETTE'S U'S REPORTER)

Alex Chamberlain
Greg Halford
Wayne Brown
Tony English
Nicky Smith
Mark Kinsella
Steve McGavin
Kevin Watson
Lomana Tresor Lua Lua
Perry Groves
Tony Adcock

Subs: Aidan Davison (g), Tony McCarthy (d), Alan White (d), Gavin Johnson (m), Richard Wilkins (m), Colin Hill (m), Steve Whitton (f).

I have chosen these players in a 4-4-2 formation.

ALEC CHAMBERLAIN – played in goal between 1983-87 before he was transferred to Everton for £80,000. Very reliable between the sticks.

GREG HALFORD – powerful performer at fullback and very comfortable playing further up field. Transferred to then Premier League Reading for £2.5 million.

WAYNE BROWN – all-action hardman in the heart of defence.

TONY ENGLISH (my captain) – comfortable playing anywhere in the team.

NICKY SMITH – attacking fullback. Good defender who loved to be let loose on the left.

MARK KINSELLA – two good feet. Another player who is happy anywhere in the team.

STEVE McGAVIN – very exciting ball skills and scorer of some great goals. The former Sudbury Town midfielder quickly caught the eye of Birmingham City manager Barry Fry who took the U's favourite to St Andrews for a transfer fee of £150,000.

KEVIN WATSON – the quality of his early life at Tottenham Hotspur always shone through.

LOMANA TRESOR LUA LUA – always exciting to watch, played without fear.

PERRY GROVES – a snip for a club like Arsenal at £50,000.

TONY ADCOCK – top quality striker who deserved his chance to play in higher League football. Transferred to Manchester City for £75,000 in 1987.

SUBS:

AIDAN DAVISON (g) – experienced keeper who

invoked great confidence in his team-mates in front of him.

TONY McCARTHY (d) – good solid defender. Joined the U's from Millwall before returning to Shellbourne in his native Republic of Ireland.

ALAN WHITE (d) – no nonsense central defender who always gave everything. Played with his heart on his sleeve.

GAVIN JOHNSON (d/m) – solid and reliable either in defence or midfield.

RICHARD WILKINS (m/d) – good player capable of performing anywhere on the pitch.

COLIN HILL (d/m) – Northern Ireland international whose class shone through until he was stolen by Sheffield United for £40,000 following a Football League tribunal.

CHAPTER 37
MEET THE CHAIRMEN

Only four men held the post of Colchester United chairman during my role as the *Evening Gazette*'s U's correspondent. One of them was rich, loud and outspoken, two were wealthy, modest and quietly spoken, while the other was a local builder with blue and white striped blood flowing through his veins.

They were, in order of sequence; Jonathan Crisp, James Bowdidge, Gordon Parker and Peter Heard.

JONATHAN CRISP – the big, brash South African millionaire waltzed into Layer Road in May 1985 with the boast, "I'm going to take this club up into the Second Division!" (today's Sky Bet Championship). As things turned out he achieved completely the opposite by chairing the U's out of the Football League into the GM Vauxhall Conference.

He managed to upset the fans by introducing a disastrous 100 per cent membership scheme to watch matches and he installed Mike Walker as manager in April 1986, only to controversially sack him nineteen months later.

He replaced Walker with the equally controversial, but relatively unknown, Roger Brown on the recommendation of ex-Arsenal double-winning manager Bertie Mee. Brown was to bring his more strict, industrial management skills into the dressing room. A move that failed badly.

Crisp always had three or four hangers-on with him and, at my first meeting, he said, "Watch out boys here comes the press."

I thought quickly and replied, "Where would you be without us? What other business gets a free advert on the back of our paper every night?" My comment clearly rang a bell with the big man and we got on like a house on fire after that.

I remember him one day when I went to the club and the U's were languishing near the bottom of the Fourth Division table. He told me that the players' representatives, Dale Tempest and Ian Allison, didn't like what I was writing and wanted me banned from the ground. Jonathan said I told them to bugger off and play much better so I couldn't write anything bad about them.

I also remember him on the last day of the 1989-90 season. The U's were already condemned to Conference football when Burnley beat them. Jonathan was expecting a big backlash from the fans because the U's had been relegated out of the League. Instead, it was the Burnley fans who invaded the Layer Road pitch demanding the head of their manager, Frank Casper.

However, the larger than life, ever controversial Crisp saved the best for last. On the day he handed over the club to fellow director James Bowdidge, I knew all was not well with him so I waited until the cameras stopped whirring and all the other journos had gone before asking him, "What's the chairman really feeling today?"

He let rip a tirade of abuse towards those who he said had been scheming behind his back.

Totally pissed off by all the back-biting, he proclaimed, "The king is dead, long live the king!"

He then unleashed a sensational display of passion and bitterness against those he said have been trying to bring him down, saying, "I would just like to express my contempt for those people who call themselves loyal supporters, but go around tearing down all the foundations. They wanted Crisp out and now they've got it."

As he walked away from Layer Road for the last time he said: "I am more than happy for those people to come forward, stand up and be counted."

JAMES BOWDIDGE – the fan who was now in charge.

Twelfth-man for the Boys High School Under-11 cricket team; anchor-man for the Colchester Young Farmers tug-of-war team; super-sub for the St Quintin Football team and the ninth-best grouse shot in the country, the thirty-year-old City merchant banker; local farmer and founder of the Property Merchant Group 1992, promptly declared: "I'm now giving the U's back to the people!"

The grandson of former U's chairman Harold Moore, James said: "I will be launching a shares scheme to give Colchester United Football Club a wider ownership. The continued survival of Colchester United now very much depends on them."

Business commitments meant he could not devote as much time to the club as he would have liked and, at the end of his first and only season, he asked Colchester man Peter Heard, a fellow property developer, to buy into the club.

James did have the honour of being chairman for what emerged as a fantastic season, bowing out with a triumphant GM Vauxhall Conference championship and FA Trophy winning double, plus a historic first trip to a Wembley final.

GORDON PARKER – local builder and Colchester United fanatic.

Gordon, a former U's reserve team player, was more of a figurehead than a financial backer. Although Peter Heard owned the majority of shares, he was happy to remain in the background and let Parker assume the mantle of chairman.

Mr Parker was more than willing to discuss club affairs with the media and he really got into close quarters with me in a game at Halifax when he ran over my foot when attempting to park his Jaguar.

Gordon had already served two separate spells on the board and he eventually handed the chairman's reins over to Peter Heard at the celebration dinner following the U's Division Three Play-Off final victory at Wembley.

PETER HEARD – quiet man, private man, big wallet!

I have already spoken elsewhere in this book of my sometimes volatile relationship with Mr Chairman. However, I am happy to add if you were an employee of his all your details remained a secret. He would never discuss transfer fees, or a player's terms of his contract. We always had to try and get those figures from other sources.

Peter can claim to have overseen several big money transfers like the £2.25 million from Newcastle for Lomana Tresor Lua Lua; the £2.5 million deal from Reading for Greg Halford and the £850,000 sale of Jamie Cureton to Norwich City.

On the bleaker side he found himself embroiled in a costly lawsuit involving former U's manager George Burley and an equally costly lawsuit involving U's player Brian Launders and his agent, Barry Silkman.

Peter had long dreamed of the club performing in a new stadium and played a major role in what is now the U's new home at the Weston Homes Community

Stadium.

He stepped down in September 2006 and sold his controlling shares to Tiptree-based Jobserve millionaire Robbie Cowling.

CHAPTER 38
PETER WRIGHT REMEMBERED

One of the greatest thrills of my most recent years has been the creation and subsequent emergence of the Colchester United Football Club's Former Players Association – Peter Wright's baby!

Peter – voted by *Colchester Gazette* readers as the U's Player of the 20th Century – sadly died in October 2012, but not before he had seen his long-time dream of the CUFCFPA become a reality.

The dazzling former Layer Road favourite spent hours in the *Gazette* office seeking information about other clubs' former players' set-ups and I was proud to say yes when he asked me if I would help him get the U's FPA off the ground.

I wrote letters for him to here, there and everywhere and most of the responses were very encouraging. Our Friday afternoon trip to neighbouring Ipswich Town proved very fruitful. Town's former player Simon Milton couldn't have been more helpful. Preston North End and Hull City were also magnificent in their responses too, but all we got from mega rich Manchester United was the offer of a signed football!

Peter was like a dog with a bone where his CUFCFPA dream was concerned. He left no stone unturned in his quest to get it off the ground.

I was so glad that he, as its inaugural chairman, was able to enjoy several annual dinners before he sadly passed away. Regretfully, because of certain circumstances, I was forced to drop by the wayside, but the larger than life John Schultz stepped in and quickly got things moving. In no time at all Peter and John set the ball rolling and before we knew it we were all enjoying the first annual dinner.

Peter would be so proud to see his dream thriving as it is today and thanks to his good friend, John Schultz, the CUFCFPA looks set to thrive for many years to come.

CHAPTER 39
GOOD TIMES – BAD TIMES

No Prize for Witts

'YOU CANNOT BE SERIOUS!' Read the *Evening Gazette* back page headline.

U's boss Steve Whitton had just topped the table as the Nationwide Division Two Manager of the Month for August 2001 – but the sponsors handed the award to Bristol City manager Danny Wilson instead.

What a cock-up!

Both Whitts and Wilson remained unbeaten in August, but the U's manager's record was better because of the quality of the opposition the U's played.

Hoddle Taught Wright a Lesson

Professional footballers are only too ready to hog the limelight when everything is going well for them! But how many of them give something back?

A perfect example of that involved former England footballers Glenn Hoddle and Ian Wright.

Former Arsenal star striker Wright was coming towards the end of his career when he played for Burnley against the U's at Layer Road in February 2000. Naturally, the kids flocked round him before the game, thrusting their many books at him to autograph. But he told them he didn't have time to do it then and to all come back to the dressing room tunnel at the end of the game when he would do the honours for them. The kids waited and waited, but there was no sign of Wright. He had slipped away out of a back exit to leave them all frustrated and unhappy.

It sickens me every time I see him spouting his big gob off as a TV football pundit now.

With Hoddle it was a completely different story. Glenn was player-manager of Chelsea at the time and when the kids flocked round him before a pre-season friendly at Colchester he told them come out to the centre-circle after the match and I'll give you all my autograph then. True to his word he marched out to the middle, organised the kids into a respectable queue and duly did the business – every last one!

What a difference and what a gentleman – well done Glenn!

What's in a Name?

Did you know former U's player-manager Roy McDonough was actually meant to be christened Jane Elizabeth?

The 'Big Fella's' mum, Iris, already had two boys – Jim and Keith – and was desperate for a girl when our Roy came along. Roy was born the second of twin boys and when his brother popped out first mum immediately named him Gary. Confident that her fourth child had to be a girl, Mum McDonough up in Solihull quickly replied, "Jane Elizabeth," when asked what her next child was going to be called!

Is that why Roy was always called a "Big Girl's Blouse" by away supporters everywhere?

Sage and Onion Superstition

Superstition and football have gone hand in hand from the moment ragamuffins began kicking a rolled up rag around the streets of Colchester.

There wasn't a rabbit's foot or four-leaf clover anywhere in sight when fanatical U's supporter Kathy

Warner revealed to the *Gazette* before a certain away trip that her formula for success came in the shape of two packets of Sage and Onion stuffing. She informed her dad – another lifelong U's fan – over a chicken lunch the day before the match, that if they didn't polish off all the stuffing by midnight the U's were sure to lose the next day.

As the witching hour approached there was still oceans of the stuffing, now cold and stodgy, left. So, fearing the worst, Kathy and dad got stuck in again. Everybody lived happily ever after – the U's well and truly stuffed their rivals 4-0 – but only because dad wore his lucky trousers!

How's That For Loyalty!

Some people will go to any lengths to follow their favourite team up and down and across the country.

I've heard of some incredible instances of loyalty, but the three Colchester United fans who made a midweek journey to watch their team in GM Vauxhall Conference action at Yeovil surely deserve a special prize!

When lottery agent Sid Grice and his fellow lifelong U's supporters, Jim and Vanessa Wilkinson, of Layer Road drew a blank after long and desperate efforts to get a place on the supporters' coach or fix-up a lift, they had only one option left – a fare of £162 for a cab all the way to the West Country and back.

News of their 400-mile round trip spread quickly and the trio were given a rousing welcome by the Yeovil fans just before the players took to the field. No doubt they rounded off their day by thinking it was all worth it – their heroes won by the only goal.

Shattered and sleepy-eyed, All The Fours cab driver George Dickson summed up the day when telling the *Gazette*: "I'm ready for the Merthyr Tydfil run now!"

What Went Wrong Then?

Things couldn't have got much worse the day Hereford humbled Colchester United at Edgar Street in October 1993. The U's finished the match with only nine men and two recognised goalkeepers sent-off, plus a 5-0 thrashing to boot.

Weston-Super-Mare whistler Ron Groves became the first referee to send-off two goalkeepers from the same team – John Keeley and sub Nathan Munson – in a match, both for professional fouls.

For the record, Hereford striker Chris Pike became only the second Football League player to score a hat-trick against three different keepers – Keeley, sub Roy McDonough and second sub Munson.

Manager McDonough summed things up when saying: "It was so bizarre out there, like something out of *Beadle's About*, so many things went wrong."

Kelly's Eye

Former Football Association chief executive Graham Kelly confessed to being bowled over by Colchester United after watching them beat previous leaders Farnborough to leap to the top of the GM Vauxhall Conference table back in November 1991.

Kelly said at the time, "I see a lot of Conference matches, but this was one of the best! I thought Colchester pressed forward very well before half-time and their second half performance was excellent – they were deserving winners."

He also took time out to praise the 1,500 U's fans who made the trip to Farnborough's Cherrywood Road ground. "The fans were very enthusiastic and their behaviour was excellent," he said.

Blossoming Flowers

The word 'legend' is banded about far too readily in football and other sports these days!

But when the sentiment surrounding the word legend is said with true meaning it ain't half good for the old ego.

When checking out my Facebook account recently I came across the following message from former Colchester United defender Paul Flowers who had noticed that I was writing this book.

Paul said, "I will be buying that Francis. You were the first person I was ever interviewed by before my League debut in March 1993 (Cardiff City at Layer Road). You were a bit of a legend back then."

Guy Lands Himself in a Pickle

One-time Colchester United loanee Guy Branston had a big score to settle when he captained his then club Peterborough United against the U's in March 2004.

The 'Caveman' defender, who hogged tablespoons full of the aptly named Branston Pickle down his gullet during one of his two loan spells at Layer Road, following a promotion set-up by yours truly and Crosse & Blackwell, makers of the popular relish, told the *Gazette* he was still waiting for the U's to send him a promotion-winning medal after helping the club reach the Second Division six years earlier when he was on loan from Leicester City.

Branston said, "I also want to show the bloke who used to run around in midfield for Reading wearing a gum-shield, while trying to throw his weight, about that I am still too good for him."

That 'bloke' was U's boss Phil Parkinson and his club Reading were the chief promotion rivals to Rotherham who had snapped-up central defender Branston for £50,000 from Leicester.

He said: "Who is this guy battering my team-mates about? Is he wearing a gum-shield because he's afraid of getting a punch in the mouth? So I made sure he knew I was about."

Branston was on loan at Peterborough at the time and, sadly for him, he didn't get the better of the U's former Reading 'Gum-shield Warrior'. Ten-man Colchester battled on for a goalless stalemate after having quicksilver striker Wayne Andrews sent-off.

Marc Lives His Dream

Colchester United team coach driver Marc Marangou could not believe his luck when he was handed a chance to live a dream.

He had always wanted to play cricket for Essex! Official coach driver for the Essex County Cricket team as well, he was handed that chance when the county's captain, Ronnie Irani, asked him if he wouldn't mind carrying out the twelfth-man duties when the original named player had to return home on Friday night, leaving the team short in the event of a crisis on the last day.

The game at Northamptonshire was grinding towards a draw as it moved into the final day and Marc said: "I jumped at the chance when Ronnie asked me and I would have been very happy just taking the bottles of water out to the middle for the batsmen.

He added: "I couldn't believe it, however, when Ronnie asked me to come out and field for a couple of overs in Northants' second innings as Ravi Bopara left the field for a toilet break."

Irani said: "Marc was wearing Bopara's shirt and a pair

of James Foster's whites. The lads rustled up some other kit, so he really looked the part. He made a couple of good stops, but he needs to work harder on his throwing."

The live-wire Cedrics coach driver added, "It was a fantastic experience and I thoroughly enjoyed myself. I must be the oldest man to make a debut for the county."

Costly Principles

When Colchester United chairman Peter Heard had a bee in his bonnet he was a hard man to shift.

That tough mindset of his, however, was severely put to the test around Christmas Eve 1994 when U's manager George Burley walked out on the club to become the new team boss of Ipswich Town.

So began the George Burley saga!

Scottish international defender Burley had been a star player at the Portman Road club several years earlier, but a man of great principle, Mr Heard refused to budge when the U's lofty Suffolk neighbours eventually lured their former fans' favourite back.

The stand-off between the two East Anglian rivals resulted in an acrimonious war of words lasting nearly three years before a High Court found in Colchester's favour. Unfortunately, a large chunk of the compensation was spent on barristers' fees, but Mr Heard won the battle!

He wasn't so lucky, however, over the Brian Launders affair, a Mick Wadsworth signing who was sacked at a minute's notice one morning for gross misconduct. Irishman Launders was the only U's player never to give me his phone number and hopes were high of another Heard triumph after Launders' case for wrongful dismissal and compensation was thrown out by both the

Football Association and the Football League.

Sadly, the U's eventually had to cough up a phone number in the player's £40,000 loss of wages and costs, plus further multiple damages and legal costs to his agent, Barry Silkman, when a Civil Court judge ruled against the club at a later date.

The barristers also pocketed a small fortune, but at no time did Peter Heard and the U's board of directors shirk their principles!

Tears and Cheers for Farewell

There were tears and cheers as family members of the late Colchester United captain Bobby Cram returned to Layer Road in May 2008 to scatter his ashes.

To mark the occasion yours truly presented the family with a giant framed montage of pictures depicting the classy defender's career as a U's player.

Joy Lynch and Betty Stephenson (Bobby's sisters), along with Brenda Cram (his sister-in-law), travelled down to Colchester from the north-east where the popular late U's skipper grew up. According to his sisters, former West Bromwich Albion defender Cram enjoyed the best years of his illustrious career at Layer Road before emigrating to Canada in 1972 for a second time to become player-coach of Vancouver Spartans.

He was skipper of legendary U's boss Dick Graham's U's Grandads' giant-killing side that shocked star-studded Leeds United in the FA Cup. He also captained the side that beat his former club West Bromwich Albion at The Hawthorns to win the Watney Cup, both in 1971.

Cooking Up a Storm

Bacon butties, beans and baked spuds, scrambled eggs, pasta and sweetcorn. These tasty delights were all part of Colchester United's 'Away Day' nosh expertly dished up by lifelong supporter and 'super chef' Martyn Gosling.

Magical Martyn – the on-coach chef – was as important as the team itself back in the mid-90s when U's boss at the time Steve Wignall, drafted him into the Layer Road set-up with the illustrious title of Self-employed Catering Manager. With the cost of hotel bills soaring it was all part of a U's cost-cutting exercise to wipe-out hefty overnight hotel bills.

One of his main roles, and probably the most important, was to make sure the players were properly well fed on the long first team away trips which often started early in the morning and returned late at night.

Martyn said: "The idea was to make sure the players ate better food; the right kind of food, and when Steve Wignall asked me if I would be prepared to do it I jumped at the chance.

"I serve anything on the way to a match which is high on protein and carbo-hydrates such as pasta with chicken and sweetcorn; baked potatoes cheese and beans or scrambled egg. On the way back the lads would tuck into the odd baked spud, curry and rice, chilli, pasta, or a piping hot bowl of soup.

"It all started when youth team coach Steve Foley, worried that his young players might be gorging themselves on hamburgers, chocolates and sweets, asked me if I would come into the club at lunchtimes and make sure they ate the right kind of foods.

"It was important to have something right off the pitch and everything just snowballed from there."

Trained at Colchester's George Hotel, Martyn said, "I can do anything from burgers and chips to seven course meals; from sandwiches in the players dressing rooms to dressed salmon in the boardroom."

Wright Gets His Wings Clipped

Former Arsenal and England star striker Ian Wright had his wings clipped – after being accused of cuffing Colchester United's eagle mascot.

Wright, who was playing for Burnley against the U's in a Nationwide League Two clash, appeared to push Eddie the Eagle's beak away at the end of the match. That could have left the loud-mouthed goal-getter winging his way down to London to perch in front of the FA beaks if the hard done by eagle had lodged a formal complaint

U's press spokesman at the time, Brian Wheeler, said: "Wrighty has flown all over the world in his football career and now he's got the bird over something like this. Our mascot, Eddie, has not taken any action, even though Wrighty smacked him in the face."

The Football Association spokesman said the referee had not made a note in his report of any incident involving the mascot and they would not take any action unless they received a formal complaint.

"It just looks as though one or two people have had their feathers ruffled," he said.

Macari Blasts Heartless U's Chiefs

Legendary Manchester United, Celtic, West Ham and Scotland star Lou Macari had some harsh words for the Colchester United hierarchy when yours truly asked him if he was interested in the U's manager's job following Steve Whitton's sacking.

Despite being desperate to get back into a job following his own recent sacking as Huddersfield Town's manager, he told me the vacant U's job was "not for him."

The former Old Trafford star, who had guided

Huddersfield into the Second Division promotion play-offs only months before said: "I cringe when I see managers like Steve Whitton getting the sack. He did a miraculous job as Colchester United's manager. Whoever gets the job has a tremendous act to follow.

"There are certain clubs in the Second Division who you look at – Colchester are one – and say to yourself, they are performing wonders to stay there. Compared to clubs such as Huddersfield, Colchester are one of the minnows and they gave us one helluva game down at their place last year.

"I got the sack for taking my team into the play-offs. Steve suffered the same fate for doing a remarkable job. Looking in from the outside I would say Steve got the best out of those lads at Colchester with the resources available to him, but there are limits as to how far you can go. I know the feeling in many quarters down there was one of a team over-achieving just to stay in the division."

Ironically, untried Reading player and coach Phil Parkinson was handed his first managerial role as Whitton's successor and three years later guided the club to a historic promotion into the Championship.

Happy Times

It's always a great feeling when you know you've brought happiness into somebody's life. I had that feeling in a big way with the joy I brought into the lives of three Colchester United mums.

The first one was the mum of young David Hadrava who had just made his first team debut in a 2-1 LDV Vans Trophy defeat at Reading on 30 October, 2001. Mum Sue didn't live in Colchester and phoned me to see if I would send her a *Gazette* with a report of the match for keepsake – which I duly did.

It was a similar story for goalkeeper Dean Gerken's mum who lives in Rayleigh, near Southend. She wanted a copy containing details of young Dean's debut at Brentford in April 2004 – yours truly duly obliged again.

The most pleasing one of all, however, came via the son of the late former U's forward Ian Johnstone, who wanted any pictures of his dad to give to his grandmother living in Scotland.

Ian played only two League matches for the U's against Chesterfield (1-0) and Barnsley (2-2) between 1958-60. I found not only the match reports and pictures, but also the two programmes in my collection, plus a few reserve team doubles – including his name – I had as well. A highly excited young Mr Johnstone surprised his nan with her best Christmas present for years!

"You should have seen her face," he said. "She cried with utter delight. It was the last thing she was expecting."

Great stuff!

CHAPTER 40
MY ALL-TIME BEST U'S LINE-UP

Percy Ames	(1955-64)
George Fisher (capt)	(1955-60)
Brian Hall	(1965-73)
Mark Kinsella	(1986-96)
Duncan Forbes	(1961-68)
Bob Dale	(1954-57)
Sammy McLeod	(1955-62)
Lomana Lua Lua	(1998-2000)
Perry Groves	(1981-86)
Bobby Svarc	(1972-75)
Peter Wright	(1952-64)

Subs: Mike Walker (g) (1973-87), Bobby Cram (d) (1970-72), Wayne Brown (d) (2004-07), Kevin Watson (m) (2004-08), Tony Adcock (f) (1981-87).

I have selected my team to play in the original 2-3-5 formation before all the coaches came along with their variations – 4-4-2, 4-2-4, 3-5-2, 5-3-1-1, 4-3-2-1, 4-5-1 and 4-4-1-1.

PERCY AMES – the U's have fielded around sixty goalkeepers since they were first elected into the Football League and Percy is the best of them. Signed from Tottenham Hotspur, he was agile, athletic, consistent and very reliable with a truly safe pair of hands. Percy made 423 League and cup appearances for the U's.

GEORGE FISHER – equally at home at right or left back and equally skilled with either foot, George was not only the wise old head, he is also my captain. His reading of the game and sheer downright competitiveness made him one of the toughest defenders in his playing days.

BRIAN HALL – signed from Mansfield Town as a left-winger, quicksilver Brian was at his most potent relishing in all the extra space along the left flank, following his switch to play as an attacking left-back.

MARK KINSELLA – skilful and attacking wing-half or midfielder, the tasty, all-action Dubliner is one of the finest signings the U's ever made. Able to play almost anywhere from right-back to left-winger, it came as no surprise to me when he won full international honours with the Republic of Ireland.

DUNCAN FORBES – 'Thou shalt not pass' was big Duncan's motto, whether in first team action or on the training ground. A tough competitor in every way, the Edinburgh born central defender quickly became a Layer Road cult hero as he imposed his superiority over opposing strikers. I would have loved to have seen Duncan and Roy McDonough in opposition!

BOB DALE – this classy wing-half rapidly made a name for himself following his transfer from Bury. He would have definitely gone on to much better things if his professional footballing career had not been tragically cut short by contracting tuberculosis in May 1957.

PERRY GROVES – electrifying wide man who came through the U's ranks from an apprentice. Perry was transferred to top English club Arsenal for £50,000 in September 1986. Gunners manager at the time George

Graham told me he could work wonders with young Perry's pace.

SAMMY McCLEOD – genius is a very often overused word when describing some players, but in Sammy's case there was no better adjective to describe a truly gifted player. Small in stature, but massive in ball skills and vision, the tricky little Scotsman's attacking midfield flair would have been worth millions in today's transfer market.

BOBBY SVARC – his close control, quick turns and sharp shooting made the former Leicester City and Boston striker a huge favourite with the U's fans. Bobby could trap a chest-high ball, turn and shoot or pass quicker than anyone else I know.

LOMANA TRESOR LUA LUA – the most explosive player I have ever witnessed in a U's shirt. What Lomana could do with a football at his feet was absolutely mind-boggling. His silky skills earned him a lucrative £2.25 million transfer to north-east giants Newcastle United.

PETER WRIGHT – voted the *Gazette* readers Player of the Century, Colchester born Peter's dazzling runs on the left-wing caused havoc among the opponents' defence. Naturally left-footed, with a wicked turn of pace, Peter left many opponents for dead before cutting in on goal or whipping over a telling cross. He made 448 League and cup appearances for the U's.

SUBS:

MIKE WALKER (goalkeeper) – consistently good and

very reliable last line of defence. Mike, a Wales Under-23 international, made 522 League and cup appearances for the U's.

BOBBY CRAM (right-back) – cultured defender and captain of the U's famous FA Cup giant-killing team that beat mighty Leeds United in 1971.

WAYNE BROWN (central defender) – solid and dependable kingpin at the heart of defence, Wayne always left everything out on the pitch.

KEVIN WATSON (midfield) – one of the key components in manager Phil Parkinson's League One promotion-winning squad in 2005-06. Stylish midfielder Kevin started life in the Tottenham Hotspur academy.

TONY ADCOCK (forward) – 'the Red Rooster strikes again' was the cry as red-headed goal-getter Tony scored again and again. He had an uncanny knack of making a vital half-a-yard of space anywhere near the opponents' goal area before cracking the ball into the net.

FOOTBALL

Football - the beautiful and simple game I grew-up with and loved from the moment I kicked my first ball!

Sadly, it is also the beautiful and simple game I have become increasingly disillusioned with because of the obscene salaries and ever mounting rediculously over-priced transfer fees; greedy interfering agents; pontificating referees; over hyped foreign managers and players - plus the fact our game has become the plaything of multi-millionaires - most of them foreign.

It is also the beautiful and simple game that has been ruined by coaches and meddling rule-makers whose continual tampering with the action has made it a far less spectacle to watch.

It has become the beautiful and simple game that has distanced the players from the fans who worship them.

Our beautiful and simple game and, the players, have become too precious, like tin gods, who feel it and they are above everything else, while everyone looking on from the grandstands are idiots who know nothing about football!

Over-rated players, many of whom are not fit to lace the boots of such yester-year greats as Sir Stanley Matthews, Tom Finney, Billy Wright, Tommy Lawton, Len Shackleton, Wilf Mannion, Danny Blanchflower and the great crowd-pleaser George Best, have become multi-millionaires overnight with multi-million pound mansions and a fleet of top of the range cars to show-off in.

Many of today's professional footballers couldn't give a damn for the supporters who idolise them and many of today's clubs are more interested in sucking-up to sponsors and filling their corporate boxes with prawn sandwich munchers and champagne swilling no-nothings than making the game more accessible to the average fan.

Luckily, the Colchester United I grew older with was always a family club - A CLUB OF THE FANS - a club previous chairman such as Jack Rippingale, Gordon Parker, James Bowdidge and Peter Heard were all so proud and determined to keep that way!

THE AUTHOR

Francis Ponder was born in 1944, the third of four brothers, in his grandparents' tiny cottage in the Essex village of Tolleshunt D'Arcy. Francis attended Maldon Secondary School (today's Lower Plume School) at the age of eleven, moving to the newly built Tiptree County Secondary School (now Thurstable School) two years later.

Following redundancy, Francis joined the Colchester Evening Gazette in 1981, becoming the newspaper's county cricket correspondent, going on to enjoy a long career as a football reporter, commenting on the highs and lows of Colchester United. During his twenty-eight years with the paper, Francis witnessed three Wembley finals, two promotions and two relegations at the club.

A keen sportsman, Francis played Saturday football until the ripe old age of thirty-seven, despite suffering a severe cruciate ligament injury in his late twenties, representing several local clubs over the years. He also played cricket as a wicket-keeper/batsman for Tollesbury until well into his forties.

Francis has two grown up children, Jamie and Marie, and lives with his partner Joanna Wright, and their dog, Finley, in Tolleshunt D'Arcy.

www.apexpublishing.co.uk